MY First MEALS

MY First MEALS

Fast, fun recipes for children with just five ingredients

Grace Mortimer

Contents

Introduction

Why wouldn't my son eat vegetables?! I can cook. I eat five-a-day (most days!). Why was my baby not eating fistfuls of broccoli like all the others? Just before it disappeared into the bin, I salvaged a piece of boiled carrot and ate it. Then it occurred to me that, actually, I wasn't sure I'd have gone for that over the pasta either.

I started experimenting with all the usual suspects – like grating extra veg into a Bolognese – and it went well. I grated veg into more dishes, and that also went well. I questioned myself at some point: is this giving up? Maybe I'd resorted to labelling my child fussy and therefore I'd be doing this for the next 18 years. It felt like relinquishing my ambition of having a child who was a 'foodie' and instead I'd be one of those mums who cooked separate meals every night for my child for the foreseeable future. The conclusion I reached was, well it's working now and what you were doing before wasn't, so keep at it and you can worry about having a gourmet toddler another day!

I started writing down my successes and failures in a little notebook and I quickly realised that quite a distinct pattern was emerging. The fewer ingredients I used, the more successful the outcome. This was a bit of a lightbulb moment and paved the way for my 'five ingredients or less' approach, which I still use and encourage others to do too. The fewer ingredients you use, the less waste you have if your little one turns their nose up at it. Also, I think that children often don't like things by association: it isn't the sweet potato wedges they don't like, it's the paprika they once had them coated in, and so on.

The little notebook was a splattered, dog-eared, scruffy thing that lived in my kitchen and I'd often refer back to it until Harry's fussiness

subsided and I realised that maybe I would have that child who would go for tea at a friend's house and I wouldn't have to leave the poor mother with a list of things he wouldn't eat. Result! Maybe I'd done something good. What I'd done, of course, was just smuggle his vegetables into meals without him noticing, but he got used to the taste and eventually I no longer needed to smuggle them.

This concept of 'veggie-smuggling' as I call it, is something we all do as parents, I'm sure. There's certainly nothing revolutionary about it and, once Harry was older, it didn't occur to me that I'd done anything out of the ordinary.

Fast-forward to 2020, the year we were all plunged into a pandemic that no one saw coming, and suddenly we're all queuing outside supermarkets, wearing a mask and spending more time scrolling on our phones looking endlessly for memes to amuse us. I found the notebook and thought, 'should I share some of these recipes and see if anyone else finds them helpful?' I decided to set up an Instagram account, laughing at my own ridiculousness as I did so. However, it has grown from there and become the focus of all my days.

So, why five ingredients? I think it makes a meal mentally easier to work with. You can always add to it. But, if a dish is quick, cheap and uncomplicated, I know I'm more likely to attempt it. Children make impatient customers – the more time spent clattering around in cupboards looking for things, the more likely you are to give them a snack to keep them going. This means their tummies are half-full by the time you eventually present them with the culinary masterpiece you've spent hours slaving over, and sadly it's often the food waste bin or floor that sees the majority of it.

How do you choose five ingredients if you want to become a stealthy veggie-smuggler yourself? First and foremost, you need the vegetable or fruit (preferably two types) that you want to smuggle, then you need something to hide it in, which is likely beige or something they enjoy: pasta, potatoes, rice, etc. Then, you need something that adds natural seasoning: spices, cheese, pesto and so on. Whether your little one is veg-phobe or not, we can never have enough nutrients.

So, why five ingredients? I think it makes a meal mentally easier to work with. You can always add to it. But, if a dish is quick, cheap and uncomplicated, I know I'm more likely to attempt it.

These meals involve minimal ingredients and effort, while ensuring maximum goodness and flavour, giving you plenty of time to relax with that cold cup of tea you've microwaved three times...

There's nothing unusual about these veg-packed dishes, it's just often the case that if they can't see it, they can't pick it out. The goal is to get children used to the flavour/s and then the need to smuggle becomes redundant.

There is a great sense of accomplishment when successful veggie-smuggling has taken place (i.e. your tiny critic hasn't noticed said veggies) and if you are anything like me, a small victory dance around the kitchen isn't mandatory but I personally recommend it!

It hasn't all been plain sailing coming up with this formula. Despite the simplicity of the approach, things do occasionally go wrong. I recently attempted an apple crumble and I mixed up the cinnamon and cumin jars. It was a momentary lapse in concentration and I haven't been able to stop thinking about the smell. I only had five ingredients to get right and I still managed to curry a crumble! These things happen.

I hope you enjoy this collection of simple dishes – so simple, in fact, you can probably execute them with a baby in one arm while pondering the question of 'do fish sleep?' as posed to you by a wild pre-schooler who's just drawn their insignia on your bathroom wall in red crayon. Whatever the state of chaos in your kitchen, thinking up healthy recipes or measuring and weighing out ingredients doesn't have to be stressful. You probably already have most of the basics in your cupboards to make half of the dishes and you certainly won't be breaking the bank to execute the rest.

Shopping
List

Cupboard

- Eggs
- Plain Flour
- Self-Raising Flour
- Low-Salt or Zero-Salt Stock Cubes
- Wheat Biscuits (*such as Weetabix*)
- Peanut Butter
- Pasta
- Couscous
- Porridge Oats
- Mushy Peas
- Baked Beans
- Chopped Tomatoes
- Tomato Purée
- Pesto
- Coconut Milk
- Mango Chutney
- Cocoa Powder
- Chocolate
- Dried Fruit (*sultanas, raisins, apricots, etc.*)
- Reduced-Salt Soy Sauce
- Tinned Tuna or Salmon
- Dried herbs and spices (*oregano, cinnamon, paprika, mild curry powder, etc.*)

Fridge

- Cheddar Cheese
- Cream Cheese
- Milk
- Plain Yoghurt
- Non-Dairy Alternatives (*as needed*)
- Mince

Fruit and Veg

- Apples
- Aubergines
- Avocados
- Bananas
- Blueberries
- Broccoli
- Carrots
- Courgettes
- Peppers
- Raspberries
- Sweet Potatoes
- Tomatoes (*cherry and regular*)

Freezer

- Peas
- Quorn
- Spinach
- Sweetcorn

Weekly
Meal Planner

	Monday	Tuesday	Wednesday
Breakfast	Banana and Peanut Butter Pancakes (page 28)	*Leftover* Strawberry Oatcakes *with yoghurt* (page 154)	wheat biscuits with and mashed bana
Savoury Snack	Bobble Patties (page 78)	*Leftover* Tuna Salad Pinwheels (page 108)	*Leftover* Carrot and Sweetco Scones *with cream ch* (page 114)
Lunch	Tuna Salad Pinwheels (page 108)	Carrot and Sweetcorn Scones (page 114)	Cheeseboard Muffi *with apple sticks* (page 106)
Sweet Snack	Strawberry Oatcakes (page 154)	Healthy Chocolate Mini Pancakes (page 142)	Peach and Aprico Flapjacks (page 14
Dinner	Veggie Lasagne *with peas* (page 184)	Quick Satay *with noodles* (page 179)	Florentine Pizza (page 194
Dessert	fruit and yoghurt	Rasberry and Chocolate Mousse (page 220)	fruit, oats and yoghu topped with a little sy

Here is an example meal plan. Don't worry – you don't have to cook 15 different meals each week! There are plenty of leftover dishes to be eaten up on subsequent days, to save you from cooking multiple times a day. While this might look like quite a lot of 'recipes' to rustle up, consider how long it takes to heat up some fish fingers or even just make a sandwich – plenty of these dishes take the same amount of time. Equally, if fish fingers or sandwiches are all you can face making occasionally, there is absolutely no judgement here! But if you're someone who likes to plan your meals, this is a useful template to follow.

I've also given you a blank template on page 232, so that you can plan out your own menus once you've worked out what works for your own little one/s. Photocopy it and stick it to your fridge for easy reference.

Thursday	Friday	Saturday	Sunday
Leftover ach and Apricot ojacks (page 144)	*Leftover* Strawberry and Vanilla Loaf *with yoghurt* (page 140)	Tomato Chia Pancakes *with grated cheese* (page 30)	Broccoli Bread *with cream cheese* (page 73)
Leftover eseboard Muffins (page 106)	*Leftover* Crispy Veggie Rolls (page 94)	Broccoli Bread (page 73)	*Leftover* Pizza Patties (page 62)
spy Veggie Rolls (page 94)	Pear and Parsnip Soup *with bread* (page 116)	Pizza Patties *with veggie sticks* (page 62)	*Leftover* Tortilla Tarts (page 101)
Strawberry and anilla Loaf Cake (page 140)	fruit salad	Cinnamon Pear Biscuits (page 134)	*Leftover* Cinnamon Pear Biscuits (page 134)
Avocado Pasta (page 171)	Campfire Stew with Baked Sweet Potatoes (page 180)	My First Curry *with rice* (page 174)	Brocciflower Cheese *with your Sunday roast* (page 120)
dgy Banana and ocolate Flapjacks (page 230)	*Leftover* Banana and Chocolate Flapjacks (page 230)	Cereal Ice Cream *with fruit* (page 202)	*Leftover* Cereal Ice Cream *with Plum Crumble* (page 209)

Notes

Portion sizes and storage

I have days where I'm ridiculously hungry for no reason and days where I'm not that bothered at all or just don't fancy the food that has been put in front of me. Well, children are much the same! On Monday you might find half a slice of toast is all your little one wants to eat for breakfast and on Tuesday you might find that even after you've served them their third bowl of porridge, the words 'I'm still hungry' echo through your kitchen and it's not even 8 a.m..

I have tried to offer rough guides on how many small people these recipes serve, but no two children are the same and what might be an ample portion of pasta for one child is simply a starter for another! That's before we've even differentiated age groups and growing appetites, so it's almost impossible to give an accurate estimate. That said, I distinctly hate throwing any food away, especially if it's something that Harry has enjoyed but I've made too much of, which is why most of these dishes are perfect to pop in the fridge and reheat for the following day, or decant into a zip-lock bag and chuck in the freezer. Cook once, eat twice, I say!

If you're anything like me – you might find you quite fancy that leftover pinwheel or muffin for yourself and then you have to blame those greedy fridge pixies for eating it. Never underestimate the memory of a hungry toddler!

Key to symbols

 Veggie

 Suitable for freezing

One

Breakfast

Breakfast

Now, if you are anything like me, breakfast most mornings consists of a hasty slice of toast for Harry while I inhale a coffee and desperately try to find a pair of matching socks! However, if you have a little more time on your hands in the morning, perhaps at the weekend, then here are a few easy ideas for something slightly more interesting. Or, if you're feeling organised, you can make them the night before and just pop them in the microwave to reheat them. There is certainly no expectation to get up an hour earlier than usual to make freshly baked muffins for your little ones... I wouldn't dream of it either!

oatmeal peach smoothie

Serves

1

This is so filling it definitely works as a meal in its own right. The more milk you add, obviously, the thinner the mixture will be, but Harry likes his smoothies thick and creamy (almost as thick as yoghurt). You can pour this over cereal or fruit for a super-duper breakfast or just pop some in a cup or bottle. I make this for Harry if he's been a bit under the weather and isn't particularly keen to sit at the table for a proper meal. It works wonders!

1 ripe peach

2 tbsp porridge oats

1 tbsp full-fat yoghurt (ideally Greek-style)

a splash of milk (any type)

pinch of ground cinnamon (optional)

1. Destone the peach and slice it into chunks. Add it to a food processor or blender along with the oats, yoghurt and milk. Blitz until smooth.

2. Pour into a glass and enjoy! Add a sprinkle of cinnamon on top, if you wish.

Breakfast

blueberry and vanilla pancakes

Makes

8

pancakes

serves 4
toddlers
or 2 older
children

What's not to love? These are very versatile. For those who don't eat eggs, the egg can swapped for chia egg (see Tip), and the blueberries can be swapped for raspberries or strawberries, but there's something about the colour of blueberry pancakes that makes them so beautiful, especially when they are drizzled with some glistening syrup – yum!

1 cup (130g) self-raising flour

1 cup (250ml) milk (any type)

1 egg

1 handful of blueberries

1 tsp vanilla extract

For cooking
drizzle of sunflower oil

1. Combine all the ingredients, except the oil, in a bowl and beat thoroughly until well combined.

2. Heat a drizzle of oil in a frying pan over a medium heat. Add ladle-sized amounts of the mixture to the frying pan and fry on each side for a couple of minutes until golden.

3. Serve immediately, with more blueberries and a drizzle of extra syrup if you wish.

4. Fine to freeze. To cook from frozen, allow the pancakes to defrost naturally, then reheat in the microwave or in a dry frying pan.

To make a chia egg, simply mix 1 level tablespoon of chia seeds with 2 tablespoons of water and set aside for 10 minutes to allow the chia seeds to swell and become jelly-like in consistency. Add it to the pancake mixture, as you would an egg.

banana and peanut butter pancakes

Makes
8–10 small pancakes

serves
2 toddlers
or 1 older
child

I'm hard pushed to think of a more perfect combo than banana and peanut butter, so it makes even more sense to turn it into pancakes. The first time I made these, Harry told me it was the best breakfast he'd ever had. Well, if that's not a ringing endorsement, I don't know what is! These are lovely with a blob of extra peanut butter and some chopped bananas on top.

1 banana, plus extra to serve

1 tbsp peanut butter (any type), plus extra to serve

1 cup (100g) porridge oats

1 cup (250ml) milk (any type)

1 egg

For cooking
drizzle of sunflower oil

1. In a bowl, mash the banana and peanut butter together, then add the oats, milk and the egg and mix thoroughly.

2. Heat a drizzle of oil in a frying pan over a medium heat. Add the mixture in ladle-sized amounts to the pan and fry on each side for a couple of minutes until golden.

3. Serve with some extra peanut butter on top and a few slices of banana, if you like.

4. Fine to freeze. To cook from frozen, allow the pancakes to defrost naturally, then reheat in the microwave or in a dry frying pan.

Breakfast

tomato chia pancakes

Makes
8–10 small
pancakes

serves
2 toddlers
or 1 older
child

Chia seeds are bloomin' amazing things! These pancakes are so delicious and super fluffy – you just can't go wrong with them. If you don't have chia seeds, you can of course swap them for an egg and the recipe still works perfectly, but I'd encourage you to have a go with chia seeds because they are full of fibre and minerals. An all-round great start to the day!

1 cup (130g) self-raising flour

1 cup (250ml) milk (any type)

1 tbsp chia seeds

3 tbsp tomato purée

1 handful of grated cheese (any type)

For cooking
drizzle of sunflower oil

1. Combine all the ingredients, except the oil, in a bowl and beat thoroughly. Leave to stand for 5 minutes to allow the chia seeds to swell.

2. Heat a drizzle of oil in a frying pan over a medium heat.

3. If the mixture is too thick to ladle into the pan, add a splash of milk to loosen it.

4. Add ladle-sized amounts of the mixture to the frying pan and fry on each side for a couple of minutes until golden.

5. Serve immediately.

6. Fine to freeze. To cook from frozen, allow the pancakes to defrost naturally, then reheat in the microwave or in a dry frying pan.

Breakfast

sweet potato pancakes

Makes

8

Whatever the day throws at you, these make an extremely healthy and filling breakfast for any or all members of the family. These are lovely with a little peanut butter drizzled over them.

1 sweet potato

2 tbsp self-raising flour

2 tbsp porridge oats

1 egg

For cooking
drizzle of sunflower oil

1. Preheat the oven to 200°C (180°C fan).

2. Prick the sweet potato a few times with the tip of a knife and bake it for 45 minutes, or until it is nice and soft.

3. Halve the baked sweet potato, scoop the flesh out of the skin into a bowl, mash and leave to cool.

4. Once the mash is cool, add the flour, oats and egg and mix thoroughly.

5. Heat a drizzle of oil in a frying pan over a medium heat. Add tablespoon-sized amounts of the potato mixture and fry for a few minutes on each side until golden brown.

6. Remove to a plate lined with kitchen paper and pat off any excess oil.

7. Serve immediately.

 These can be kept for up to up to 48 hours in a sealed container, or on a plate covered with clingfilm, in the fridge. To cook from frozen, allow the pancakes to defrost naturally, then reheat in the microwave or in a dry frying pan.

omelette roll-ups

Serves

1–2

I love omelettes, but they can be a little fiddly to get out of the pan and often the more toppings you add, the harder they are to get onto the plate without resembling scrambled eggs. Well, my dear little tortillas, we have a solution! This makes a super-speedy breakfast (or even a lunch) and is best eaten hot – I don't recommend freezing these.

2 eggs

1 avocado, peeled and de-stoned

1 tbsp cream cheese

1 tortilla wrap

For cooking
drizzle of sunflower oil

1. Beat the eggs in a bowl and set aside.

2. In a separate bowl, mash together the avocado and cream cheese, then spread it all over one side of the tortilla wrap.

3. Heat a drizzle of oil in a frying pan over a medium heat. Pour the egg into the frying pan and tilt the pan until it covers the whole base, then pop the tortilla on top of the egg (dry side down). Cook for a few minutes until the egg is set, then remove from the pan to a plate.

4. Roll up the tortilla, then slice it into discs and serve immediately.

melt-in-the-middle muffins

Makes

6

These muffins have melted cheese in the middle. Need I say more?!

3 handfuls of spinach

1 cup (130g) self-raising flour

4 tbsp milk (any type)

3 eggs

6 small cubes of Cheddar cheese

For greasing
butter or sunflower oil

1. Preheat the oven to 200°C (180°C fan). Grease a 6-hole muffin tin with a little butter or oil.

2. Finely chop the spinach and place it a bowl along with the flour, milk and eggs. Beat thoroughly to break up any lumps.

3. Pour the mixture into the holes of the muffin tin and push one cube of cheese into the middle of each muffin.

4. Bake for 30 minutes.

5. Remove from the oven and leave to cool slightly before popping them out to enjoy.

6. Fine to freeze. Defrost naturally and reheat in the microwave or pop them in a 200°C (180°C fan) oven for 10 minutes.

avocado and feta pancakes

Makes 8–10 small pancakes

serves 2 toddlers or 1 older child

I don't know if you've become a member of the savoury pancake appreciation club, but if you're on the fence, then I implore you to try making these and reconsider! These are full of brilliant healthy fats; they can be drizzled with syrup and served with chopped fresh fruit (fresh figs are our favourite, if you can find them and are feeling decadent!) or can be plated up just as they are. Feta cheese is obviously quite salty, so if you plan to serve these to babies under 1 year old, either omit it, swap it for cream cheese or just add a little less.

1 avocado, peeled and de-stoned

1 cup (250ml) milk (any type)

1 egg

1 cup (130g) self-raising flour

a few cubes of feta cheese

For cooking
drizzle of sunflower oil

1. Mash the avocado in a bowl and add the milk, egg and flour. Crumble in the feta cheese and mix together – the mixture doesn't need to be completely smooth.

2. Heat a drizzle of oil in a frying pan over a medium heat. Ladle in small amounts of the mixture and fry each pancake for about 3 minutes on each side until golden. They are ready to flip when bubbles start to form on the top side.

3. Serve warm.

4. Fine to freeze. To cook from frozen, allow the pancakes to defrost naturally, then reheat in the microwave or in a dry frying pan.

baked bean waffles

Yes, you read that right! And, yes, they are this bright! The first time I made these and shared the recipe online, the feedback was unbelievable. Baked beans are marvellous but they can be a little messy just served on their own. When cooked like this, however, they break down and become almost creamy. You just have to try it for yourself.

about 4 tbsp tinned baked beans

1 tbsp plain yoghurt

3 tbsp self-raising flour

1 handful of grated cheese (any type)

1 tbsp tomato purée

For greasing
butter or sunflower oil

1. Preheat the oven to 200°C (180°C fan). Prepare a silicone waffle mould (about 18.5 x 18.5 x 1.5cm) or grease a 6-hole muffin tin with a little butter or oil.

2. Mix all the ingredients together in a bowl until well combined. Spoon the mixture into the waffle mould or muffin tin.

3. Bake for 30 minutes.

4. Remove from the oven and leave until nearly cool before popping them out to serve.

5. Fine to freeze. To cook from frozen, defrost naturally, then reheat in the microwave for 30 seconds.

You can, of course, use a waffle iron to cook these. Grease it beforehand and follow the manufacturer's instructions. You will find that they cook much more quickly, and you may need to loosen the mixture with a little extra milk.

Breakfast

stuffed hash browns

Makes 6

You can't go wrong with the occasional hash brown, so these are a great idea for a weekend family breakfast. There's some hidden veg in these and you can, of course, add extra of your own (for example, sweetcorn or finely diced peppers work really well here, too). If your little one can't have egg, you don't actually need it – it just binds the whole thing together nicely. If you are omitting the egg, just mix all the remaining ingredients together and squash down firmly into well-greased muffin moulds and bake for 40 minutes.

1 baking potato

1 handful of chopped spinach

1 handful of grated cheese (any type)

1 egg, beaten

For greasing
butter or sunflower oil

1. Preheat the oven to 200°C (180°C fan). Grease a 6-hole muffin tin with a little butter or oil.

2. Grate the potato (no need to peel), then use some kitchen paper to pat down the potato to soak up some of the excess water. Pack the potato into the holes of the muffin tin and make a well in the middle of each one with your finger.

3. Bake for 10 minutes.

4. Remove the tin from the oven and divide the spinach and cheese among each hash brown, pushing it into the wells you made earlier. Divide the beaten egg equally between them and pop them back in the oven as quickly as you can to bake for another 30 minutes.

5. Serve straight from the oven.

6. Fine to freeze. These can be cooked straight from frozen in a 200°C (180°C fan) oven for 15 minutes.

baked bean muffins

Makes
6

I'm trying to remember the last time I DIDN'T have half an opened tin of baked beans in my fridge! This is a great way to use them up and they can be enjoyed on their own or cut into chunks with a little cream cheese spread over them. Either way, you'll never need to throw those abandoned half tins of beans away again.

½ x 400g tin of baked beans

1 cup (130g) self-raising flour

2 eggs

1 handful of grated cheese (any type)

1 cup (250ml) milk (any type)

For greasing
butter or sunflower oil

1. Preheat the oven to 200°C (180°C fan). Grease a 6-hole muffin tin with a little butter or oil.

2. Combine all the ingredients in a jug, then pour the mixture equally among the holes of the muffin tin.

3. Bake for 45 minutes.

4. Remove from the oven and leave to cool slightly before popping them out.

5. Fine to freeze. To cook from frozen, defrost naturally, then reheat in the microwave for 20–30 seconds.

mini baked bean omlettes

Makes
8

Continuing the theme of abandoned half-eaten tins of baked beans, here is another super simple idea to use them up. With just two main ingredients, this is a total crowd-pleaser and costs just pennies to make. As well as for breakfast, these are great for a super quick and easy lunch. We like to serve them with some grated cheese on top and some ketchup for dipping.

2 eggs

½ x 400g tin of baked beans

For cooking
drizzle of sunflower oil

1. Mix together the eggs and beans in a bowl.

2. Heat a good drizzle of oil in a frying pan over a low–medium heat. Add the mixture in tablespoon-sized amounts and fry on both sides for a few minutes until set.

3. That's it!

4. Fine to freeze. To cook from frozen, defrost naturally, then reheat in the microwave for 20–30 seconds.

cheesy cereal muffins

Makes

6

Cheese and cereal... What?! Please don't be put off by what sounds like a truly bizarre combination, because you'll be missing out on these lovely muffins. Think of the wheat bicuits as being like breadcrumbs with less salt and more fibre. Now, perhaps, this recipe doesn't seem as strange to you as it once did. These are so moist and delicious, you'll just have to trust me on this and give them a go for yourself!

1 courgette

1 wheat biscuit
(such as Weetabix)

2 handfuls of grated cheese (any type), plus 6 extra cubes of cheese for topping (optional)

2 eggs

For greasing
butter or sunflower oil

1. Preheat the oven to 200°C (180°C fan). Grease a 6-hole muffin tin with a little butter or oil.

2. Grate the courgette into a bowl and crumble in the wheat biscuit. Add the grated cheese and eggs and mix thoroughly.

3. Spoon the mixture into the muffin tin and squash it down with the back of a spoon. If you like, you can also add an extra cube of cheese to the top of each muffin.

4. Bake for 35 minutes.

5. Remove from the oven and leave to cool, then serve.

6. Fine to freeze. To cook from frozen, defrost naturally, then reheat in the microwave for 20–30 seconds.

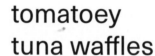

tomatoey tuna waffles

Makes

5

Serves

2

These are in the breakfast section because we traditionally think of waffles as a breakfast thing. However, they are just as good for lunch or dinner and are surprisingly filling. I enjoy them on their own but Harry insists on ketchup whenever we have them. Magical stuff is ketchup, staining children's clothes for as long as we can remember...

1 tomato or 6 cherry tomatoes, diced

3 tbsp self-raising flour

½ x 145g tin of tuna

2 tbsp tomato purée

2 eggs

1. Preheat the oven to 200°C (180°C fan).

2. Combine all the ingredients in a bowl and mix thoroughly.

3. Spoon the mixture into a silicone waffle mould (about 18.5 x 18.5 x 1.5cm) and bake for 25 minutes.

4. Remove from the oven and pop the waffle mould upside-down onto a plate. Place a spoon underneath it to let out the steam. After 20 minutes, pop the waffles out.

5. These are fine to freeze, too. I simply defrost them, then reheat in the microwave for 20 seconds.

Tip

You can, of course, use a waffle iron to cook these. Grease it beforehand and follow the manufacturer's instructions.

blueberry porridge pies

Makes

6

These are soft and squidgy, with a burst of fruit inside. They make a comforting start to the day and are a considerably less messy way to serve porridge (which, as we all know, turns to concrete if left to go cold!). If you're in a rush, these are great for breakfast on-the-go or alternatively are very nice dipped in thick, full-fat yoghurt mixed with a few extra blueberries for good measure.

1 cup (100g) porridge oats

1 cup (250ml) milk (any type)

1 egg

1 handful of blueberries

3 tbsp apple sauce

For greasing
butter or sunflower oil

1. Preheat the oven to 200°C (180°C fan). Grease a 6-hole muffin tin with a little butter or oil or fill the holes with paper muffin cases.

2. Combine the oats, milk and egg in a bowl and mix thoroughly. Pour the mixture into the prepared muffin tin holes or cases.

3. Mash the blueberries and divide them equally between each muffin, then add an equal-sized dollop of apple sauce on top.

4. Bake for 30 minutes.

5. Remove from the oven and leave them to nearly cool before popping them out.

6. Fine to freeze. Simply defrost to eat.

Breakfast

Two

Savoury Snacks

Savoury Snacks

Usually, at some point between breakfast and lunch, a child will claim to be so hungry that they think they can't possibly survive until lunchtime, so I have devised a selection of quick and easy snacks to keep them from wavering. Blood-sugar levels certainly seem to dip about mid-morning and a little something to tide them over is often preferable to the tantrum that ensues without it. I know lots of us like to get out and about in the mornings, so plenty of these are great for popping in a zip-lock bag and shoving in your bag for emergencies (usually to be forgotten about and found three days later, or is that just me?).

crispy cauli bites

Serves

2

These are perfect finger foods and a great way to introduce a little 'spice' into a little diet. You can swap the paprika for mild curry powder or leave it out altogether and they are just as tasty. I often serve these as a veggie side dish for Harry, but they make a great snack on their own, too.

1 handful of chopped cauliflower

1 handful of grated Parmesan (or nutritional yeast)

1 tsp sweet paprika

2 tbsp sunflower oil

1. Preheat the oven to 200°C (180°C fan). Line a baking tray with baking paper.

2. Tumble the cauliflower onto the prepared baking tray and sprinkle over the Parmesan, paprika and oil. Use a spoon to toss the cauliflower pieces to ensure each one is coated in the mixture.

3. Bake for 30 minutes.

4. Remove from the oven and serve.

5. Fine to freeze. Defrost naturally and then pop them in a 200°C (180°C fan) oven on a lined baking tray to reheat.

sweet beet dip

Beetroot may stain your hands but it's just about one of the most densely nutritious things around, so I encourage you to pop your little one in a dark-coloured top and let them enjoy this delicious dip. It's lovely with some veggie fingers, such as cucumber or red pepper, or used as a spread in sandwiches with cheese or shredded chicken.

2 sweet potatoes

1 x 300g pack of pre-cooked beetroot

a good glug of olive oil

1 tbsp apple cider vinegar

1. Preheat the oven to 200°C (180°C fan).

2. Bake the sweet potatoes whole for 45 minutes (or until soft inside when poked with a skewer).

3. Remove from the oven and scoop the flesh out of the potato skins. Transfer it to a blender along with the beetroot, olive oil and vinegar.

4. Blitz until smooth.

5. This keeps for up to 4 days in a sealed jar in the fridge, or freeze in an ice-cube tray and defrost as required.

pesto tortilla crisps

Serves

1

Most children love crisps, but the salt content is just a bit devastating, isn't it? However, you can very easily make your own containing just a fraction of the salt. They take just over 10 minutes to make and are so easy you could even help the children learn to make them themselves. Perfect for dipping!

1 tsp pesto

1 tortilla wrap

1. Preheat the oven to 200°C (180°C fan). Line a baking tray with baking paper.

2. Spread the pesto all over the tortilla wrap, then slice the wrap into triangular wedges like a pizza. Lay the slices on the baking tray.

3. Bake for 10 minutes.

pesto courgette bites

Pesto is a staple ingredient in our house. In fact, I think pesto pasta was my favourite comfort food as a child and Harry shares my love for it! Couscous is wonderfully quick to make and very filling, but my goodness, the mess means it's often hardly worth bothering with. This recipe is quick and delicious and, although I can't guarantee there will be no mess, it certainly limits it – they are great for little hands.

1 cup (180g) couscous

½ courgette, grated

1 tbsp green pesto

2 eggs, beaten

For cooking
drizzle of sunflower oil

1. Boil the kettle. Put the couscous in a bowl and add enough boiling water to just cover it. Cover with a plate and steam for 5 minutes.

2. Fluff the couscous with a fork, then stir through the grated courgette and set aside (this will help it cool down quicker).

3. Once the mixture has cooled to lukewarm, stir though the pesto and eggs.

4. Heat a drizzle of oil in a frying pan over a medium heat. Add tablespoon-sized amounts of the courgette mixture, flatten slightly with the back of a spatula until they are about 1cm thick, and fry for a few minutes on each side until golden.

5. Remove to a plate lined with kitchen paper to absorb any excess oil.

6. We like these dipped in a soured cream and chive dip or spread with a little cream cheese and served cold.

7. Fine to freeze or keep in the fridge for up to 2 days in an airtight container. Defrost naturally, then pop them in a 200°C (180°C fan) oven on a lined baking tray to reheat.

Savoury Snacks

pizza patties

I call these pizza patties because they taste exactly like little margherita pizzas. Granted, the ingredients list here will probably look a little obscure, but if your little one enjoys the occasional margherita pizza then you're probably safe with these.

2 wheat biscuits
(such as Weetabix)

½ x 400g tin of chopped
tomatoes

1 tsp tomato purée

1 handful of grated
cheese (any type)

4 heaped tbsp
self-raising flour

For cooking
drizzle of sunflower oil

1. Crumble the wheat biscuits into a bowl and add the remaining ingredients, except the oil. Mix until well combined.

2. Roll the mixture into balls, each about the size of a golf ball.

3. Heat a drizzle of oil in a frying pan over a medium heat. Add the balls and fry on all sides until golden and crispy (don't worry about squashing them down, they'll do so naturally).

4. Once cooked, pat them with kitchen paper to absorb any excess oil, and serve immediately.

5. Fine to freeze or keep in the fridge for up to 2 days in an airtight container. Defrost naturally and then pop them in a 200°C (180°C fan) oven on a lined baking tray to reheat.

scrumble loaf

Serves

4

In our house, we call crumpets 'scrumbles' and I'm still none the wiser as to how that came about. We also tend to find they are a 'one-a-day' type of food and given they don't last that long before going a bit soggy AND dry (they do, don't they!), this is a good way to use up those last three you have hanging about. A slice of this loaf is delicious with some cream cheese or butter thinly spread over one side. A perfect quick post-nursery/school snack.

3 crumpets

3 eggs, beaten

1 handful of sweetcorn

1 handful of chopped flat-leaf parsley

1 handful of grated cheese (any type)

1. Preheat the oven to 200°C (180°C fan). Grease and line a 22 x 10 x 6cm loaf tin with baking paper.

2. Dice the crumpets (if serving to babies under 1 year old, dice very finely into 'breadcrumbs'; otherwise into 1–2cm cubes) and add them to a bowl with the eggs. Leave to soak for 10 minutes.

3. Add the sweetcorn, parsley and cheese to the bowl and mix to combine. Pour the mixture into the prepared tin.

4. Bake for 30 minutes.

5. Remove from the oven and leave to nearly cool before popping it out and slicing it.

6. This is fine to freeze, but I advise slicing it before freezing so that you can defrost portions as and when you need them.

avocado croquettes

Do you have an avocado in the corner of your kitchen, giving you the side eye, threatening to go brown any minute now? If so, use it quickly before it delivers on its threat and make something yummy and simple. Such as these! They are lovely cold or warm and take just 10 minutes to rustle up.

1 avocado, peeled and de-stoned

½ cup (90g) couscous

1 lemon wedge

1 handful of grated Parmesan (or vegetarian hard cheese)

1. Boil the kettle.

2. Put the couscous in a bowl and add enough boiling water to just cover it. Cover with a plate and leave to steam for 5 minutes.

3. Fluff the couscous with a fork to break up any lumps.

4. In a separate bowl, mash the avocado with the juice of the lemon wedge and the Parmesan. Add the couscous and mix until well combined.

5. Using your hands, roll the mixture into croquette shapes and serve while still warm.

6. They will keep for up to 24 hours in a sealed container in the fridge. If serving from chilled, pop them on a plate lined with clingfilm and reheat for 10 seconds in the microwave, if needed.

Savoury Snacks

pea pinwheels

Serves

4–5

It wouldn't be right to give you a collection of recipes and not include my pinwheels! These are so pretty and delicious and take about 2 minutes to prepare. You can add extra sweetcorn or peas, if you wish, but we like to keep things simple and serve them like this.

1 sheet of store-bought puff pastry

1 x 300g tin of mushy peas

2 handfuls of grated cheese (any type)

For brushing
beaten egg or milk

1. Preheat the oven to 200°C (180°C fan). Line a baking sheet with baking paper.

2. Unroll the pastry sheet and spread the mushy peas over the whole sheet all the way to the outsides and corners. Sprinkle the cheese all over the mushy peas.

3. Loosely roll up the pastry sheet into a roll, then slice the roll in swift chops using a sharp knife into discs about 3cm thick. Pop the discs onto the prepared baking sheet, spacing them well apart. Brush each roll with beaten egg or milk.

4. Bake for 30 minutes.

5. Remove from the oven and let them cool for 5 minutes before lifting the pinwheels off the paper.

6. These are fine to freeze. I advise freezing them before baking between layers of baking paper. They can be baked straight from frozen (add an extra 10 minutes to the cooking time).

avocado and apricot salad with raspberry dressing

Children and salad. Not a likely duo, but don't dismiss the possibility just yet. Whether it's barbecue weather or not, this brightly coloured bowl of goodness is absolutely delicious and goes well with the finest burnt sausage or skewer around.

1 avocado, peeled and de-stoned

4 fresh ripe apricots

1 ball of mozzarella

1 handful of raspberries

a glug of olive oil

1. Slice the avocado and apricots into wedges and place them in a serving bowl.

2. Tear up chunks of the mozzarella and pop them on top of the avocado and apricots.

3. Mash the raspberries in a separate bowl with a fork. Add a glug of olive oil to the raspberries and whisk in with the fork.

4. Pour the raspberry dressing over the salad and it's ready to serve.

broccoli bread

Serves

4

Harry claims his favourite vegetable is, without doubt, broccoli. But guess what Harry almost always turns his nose up at...? Broccoli. I don't understand it either but he certainly loves a slice of broccoli bread, so perhaps this is what he means. Regardless, this makes a great snack because it's very filling and nutritious.

1 head (300g) of broccoli, finely chopped

1 handful of grated cheese (any type)

1 cup (100g) porridge oats

4 eggs

1 cup (250ml) milk (any type)

1. Preheat the oven to 200°C (180°C fan). Grease and line a 22 x 10 x 6cm loaf tin with baking paper.

2. Combine all the ingredients in a bowl and mix thoroughly. Pour the mixture into the prepared loaf tin.

3. Bake for 30 minutes.

4. Remove from the oven and leave to cool in the tin for 5 minutes, then transfer to a wire rack to cool further.

5. Slice and serve.

6. This is fine to freeze, but I advise slicing it before freezing so that you can defrost portions as and when you need them.

Tip

If you fancy vamping it up a little, add a tablespoon of pesto to the mixture as well.

sweet potato butter

Serves

4

Those lovely sweetened peanut butters are actually packed with sugar, which is why they taste so amazing. This is a great way around that problem, while adding some extra nutrients and vitamins to your child's plate when spread over a slice of toast. It can also be stirred through porridge.

2 sweet potatoes

1 tbsp unsalted butter

1 tbsp smooth peanut butter

1 tsp apple cider vinegar

1. Preheat the oven to 220°C (200°C fan).

2. Bake the sweet potatoes whole for 1 hour.

3. Once cooked, scoop the flesh out of the potato skins and place in a bowl. Leave until cool to the touch, then mix through the butter, peanut butter and vinegar until well combined. Chill until cold.

4. It will keep for up to 5 days in a sealed jar in the fridge, but can also be frozen and defrosted for use.

pea patties

I've been obsessed with mushy peas for as long as I can remember and I'm still finding new uses for them! This is one of my favourite ways to eat them and, given how cheap a tin of mushy peas is, they make for an incredibly cheap snack. A little tin goes a long way! The frozen/fresh peas bring some nice added texture.

1 cup (130g) defrosted frozen/fresh peas

½ x 300g tin of mushy peas

3 tbsp self-raising flour

1 handful of grated cheese (any type)

For cooking
drizzle of sunflower oil

1. Mix together all the ingredients, except the oil, in a bowl until well combined, then roll the mixture into balls, about the size of golf balls.

2. Heat a drizzle of oil in a frying pan over a medium heat. Add the balls to the pan and gently fry. Don't worry about flattening them into patties, they will flatten out by themselves. Fry on both sides until golden and crispy.

3. Pat them dry with kitchen paper and serve.

4. Fine to freeze. Defrost naturally and reheat in the microwave for 30 seconds, or eat cold.

carrot ketchup

Serves

4

For the 'dip-dip' obsessives out there, this ketchup is so quick and easy to whip up – you may never go back to that red variety in the glossy bottle again. Well, you might, but it's always good to try new things. This is a lovely sugar- and salt-free alternative at a fraction of the cost and goes well with just about everything. A good way to get extra veggies onto a plate.

1 x 400g tin of chopped carrots, drained
(or 1 large carrot)

1 tbsp tomato purée

1 capful/tsp red wine vinegar

1. If you're using a fresh carrot, peel, chop and boil it until it's soft, then drain.

2. Add the soft carrot chunks to a blender along with the tomato purée and vinegar and blitz until smooth. That's it!

3. This will keep for a week in a sealed jar in the fridge, or freeze in an ice-cube tray and defrost as required.

Savoury Snacks

bobble patties

Makes
7–8

These are my 'go-to' quick snacks. They are so quick, with the simplest ingredients, and as a family we all love them. I usually cook up a batch, pinch a few myself, give Harry four or five, and Tom eats the leftovers. Then everybody asks for more, so I have to make another batch... I never learn.

½ x 400g tin of baked beans

1 handful of frozen peas

1 handful of frozen sweetcorn

3 heaped tbsp self-raising flour

1 handful of grated cheese (any type)

For cooking
drizzle of sunflower oil

1. Mix together all the ingredients, except the oil, in a bowl until well combined.

2. Roll the mixture into 7–8 patties.

3. Heat a drizzle of oil in a frying pan over a medium heat. Shallow-fry the patties for 5 minutes on each side, or until golden and crispy.

4. Pat them with kitchen paper to remove any excess oil and serve.

5. Fine to freeze. Defrost naturally and reheat in the microwave for 30 seconds, or eat cold.

Savoury Snacks

herby tuna muffins

Makes

6

Getting little ones used to the flavour of fresh or dried herbs from a young age is brilliant. They don't fundamentally alter the taste of a dish, but elevate it, I think. These little muffins are packed with goodness and the batter is so easy to make, you could even make them together. These are also delicious with dill, either instead of or in addition to the parsley.

1 x 145g tin of tuna

1 avocado, peeled and de-stoned

1 handful of fresh flat-leaf parsley

2 eggs

1 handful of grated cheese (any type)

For greasing
butter or sunflower oil

1. Preheat the oven to 200°C (180°C fan). Grease a 6-hole muffin tin with a little butter or oil.

2. Drain the tuna and place in a bowl.

3. Add the avocado flesh to the bowl and mash together with the tuna.

4. Finely chop the parsley and add it to the tuna mixture along with the eggs and cheese. Mix thoroughly. Pour the mixture into the prepared muffin tin.

5. Bake for 20 minutes.

6. Remove and leave to cool slightly before popping them out of the tin.

7. Fine to freeze and just defrost naturally. Store in the fridge for up to 48 hours, covered with clingfilm or in a sealed container. These are also great for breakfast or lunch.

Savoury Snacks

guaca-mus

Combine guacamole and hummus and what do you get? I give you guaca-mus! This is simply delicious, a great little snack for those that like 'dip-dip', or used as a spread in sandwiches with some cheese or thinly sliced cucumber and ham.

1 x 400g tin of chickpeas, drained

1 avocado, peeled and de-stoned

a good glug of olive oil

juice of ½ lemon

a pinch of salt or nutritional yeast (optional)

1. Add the drained chickpeas and avocado flesh to a blender along with the olive oil, lemon juice and salt or nutritional yeast, if using. Blitz until smooth.

2. This will keep in the fridge in a sealed container for up to 4 days. It is also fine to freeze.

all-butter breadsticks

Makes

4

There are only so many cucumber fingers or carrot batons a person is willing to eat, so these are a delicious alternative. Served with a side of veggie dip or just on their own, they always go down a storm. These are actually so easy to make, you could involve your little one in the process, because the dough is quite a fun texture to make shapes out of (even if it's just rolling it into sausages). It might kill a few minutes of the day and give them something to be proud of, which (bonus) they can eat at the end.

1 cup (130g) plain flour, or as needed

4 tbsp unsalted butter, softened

2 tbsp lukewarm water, or as needed

sprinkle of sesame seeds (optional)

For brushing
sunflower oil

1. Preheat the oven to 200°C (180°C fan). Line a baking tray with baking paper.

2. Combine the flour, butter and water in a bowl and bring together to form a dough. If it is too wet, add a little extra flour; if too crumbly, add a little more water. You are looking for a quite firm but not crumbly dough; it should hold together and roll into sticks easily.

3. Divide the dough into 4 pieces and roll each piece into a long sausage. Lay them on the prepared baking tray and brush with oil. You can add a sprinkle of sesame seeds over them at this point, to add a little goodness, if you like.

4. Bake for 45 minutes.

5. That's it, they're ready to serve.

pea and bacon patties

Serves

4

Peas and bacon are a combination we know well and it just works. A little salt from the bacon, a little sweetnees from the peas, and then if you add sweetcorn – even sweeter still. Harry loves them literally swimming in ketchup but I like them just as they are! You can leave out the bacon if you wish and they are still tasty, but I'd recommend adding a little grated cheese or nutritional yeast in its place for flavour.

1 bacon rasher, chopped

½ x 400g tin of mushy peas

1 handful of sweetcorn

2 tbsp self-raising flour

1 egg

For cooking
drizzle of sunflower oil

1. Fry the bacon in a dry frying pan until crispy, then set it aside to cool for 10 minutes.

2. When cool, mix the bacon together with all of the other ingredients, except the oil for cooking, in a bowl.

3. Heat the oil in a frying pan over a medium heat. Add tablespoon-sized amounts of the mixture to the pan and fry the patties on both sides for a few minutes until golden.

4. Transfer the patties to a plate lined with kitchen paper and pat them dry and they're ready to serve.

5. These are fine to freeze. Defrost naturally and then reheat in the microwave for 20 seconds.

veggie muffins

Makes
6

Easily one of the simplest recipes in this book and yet one of the most popular ones I've ever shared. Did you know that almost all frozen veg is pre-cooked? It makes these a perfect recipe for a quick snack when your fridge is running a little low or if you haven't got the time to be chopping and steaming veggies. These are packed full of protein and, if you use a standard mixed bag of chopped veg from most supermarkets, the colour combinations make them look very pretty on a plate. Not that we have time to worry about that though!

6 tbsp any frozen veg

2 eggs

1 handful of grated cheese (any type)

For greasing
sunflower oil or butter

1. Preheat the oven to 200°C (180°C fan). Grease a 6-hole muffin tin with a little oil or butter.

2. Add a spoonful of your chosen veg to each hole of the muffin tin.

3. Whisk the eggs in a jug and divide equally between the holes, then sprinkle a little cheese on top of each one.

4. Bake for 30 minutes.

5. Remove from the oven and leave to cool slightly before popping them out.

6. Serve!

7. Fine to freeze and just defrost naturally. Store in the fridge for up to 48 hours in a sealed container.

Three

Lunchtime

Lunchtime

It never fails to amaze me how quickly lunchtime comes around. One minute you're brushing your teeth and trying to remember if you put on deodorant or not – and the next, it's midday and someone is already sitting at the kitchen table poised with a spoon, wondering when you're going to feed them! Here are some great veggie-packed meals with minimal process and ready in well under an hour (some are just 10 minutes).

crispy veggie rolls

These might look a bit fiddly to make, but they are actually really simple, and a nice shape for little hands to pick up and enjoy dipping into some yoghurt or cream cheese.

1 handful of grated carrot

1 handful of chopped kale

3 tbsp cream cheese

1 tsp green pesto

4 sheets of filo pastry

For brushing
sunflower oil

1. Preheat the oven to 220°C (200°C fan). Line a baking tray with baking paper.

2. Squeeze any excess liquid out of the grated carrot and place it in a bowl, then add the kale, cream cheese and pesto, and mix together.

3. Place 2 sheets of the filo pastry on top of each other. Cut them in half horizontally, then cut each half into 3 equal strips vertically. This should leave you with 6 equal-sized rectangles. Pop 1 tablespoon of the filling mixture onto each rectangle, then roll them up to enclose the filling as you would a spring roll, sealing them by brushing a little water onto the edges of the pastry.

4. Repeat with the other 2 sheets of filo and remaining fillling mixture, so you have 12 rolls in total.

5. Pop the rolls on the prepared baking sheet and brush them with oil.

6. Bake for 20 minutes.

7. Remove from the oven and serve hot or cold.

Lunchtime

secret cheesy garlic bread

Serves

2

The secret here is that these are secretly packed with veg, completely delicious and so easy to make! You can eat them on their own or pop a plate of them on the table to mop up any leftover pasta sauce at dinnertime.

4 heaped tbsp (40g) self-raising flour, or more as needed, plus extra for dusting

2 heaped tbsp (30g) low-fat yoghurt, or more as needed

1 handful of grated cheese (any type)

1 cube frozen spinach or 2 handfuls of fresh spinach

1 garlic clove, finely chopped

For cooking
drizzle of sunflower oil

1. Combine the flour and yoghurt in a large bowl, then stir in most of the cheese (saving a little for sprinkling on top).

2. If using frozen spinach, defrost it in the microwave for 1 minute, then drain, chop and leave to cool. If using fresh spinach, cook it in a pan of boiling water for a minute or so until wilted, then drain, chop and cool as above.

3. When the spinach is cool, add it to the bowl and knead together to form a dough. If it's too wet, add a little extra flour; if too crumbly, add a little more yoghurt until you have a nice rollable dough. Split in half and roll out with a rolling pin on a flour-dusted work surface to form 2 rough circles, about 1cm thick.

4. Heat a little oil in a frying pan over a medium heat. Add the chopped garlic and, when it is sizzling, add one of the circles of dough. Cook until golden and crispy on one side, then flip and cook the other side. Sprinkle half of the leftover cheese on top to melt while the second side is crisping up.

5. Repeat with the other circle of dough.

6. Serve immediately.

7. Fine to freeze. Defrost naturally and reheat in the microwave for 30 seconds, or eat cold.

Lunchtime

mini quiches

Makes

6

I love quiche, but trying to get Harry to eat slices of it without decorating the floor in a combination of egg and pastry is nearly impossible! Plus, there is always the issue of a soggy bottom when I make a large one (and no one wants a soggy bottom), so I find the mini ones much easier to work with. You can obviously add whatever you like to quiche, but I think creamy, cheesy spinach is so delicious, and Harry loves it, too.

1 sheet of ready-made shortcrust pastry (see Tip)

2 cubes of frozen spinach or 2 handfuls of fresh spinach

2 tbsp double cream

2 eggs

1 handful of grated cheese (any type)

1. Preheat the oven to 200°C (180°C fan).

2. Cut the sheet of pastry into 6 equal squares and line each hole in a 6-hole muffin tin with a square of pastry. Prick the bottom of each one with a fork.

3. Bake for 20 minutes.

4. Defrost the frozen spinach or cook the fresh spinach in a little boiling water until wilted, then drain and cool.

5. Place the cooled spinach in a bowl, add the double cream and eggs, then mix thoroughly. Stir in the grated cheese.

6. Remove the pastry shells from the oven and pour in the cheesy spinach mixture.

7. Bake for a further 30 minutes. Remove from the oven and leave to cool before serving.

Tip

If you don't have any ready-made store-bought shortcrust pastry, combine 125g plain flour in a bowl with 50g soft unsalted butter. Crumble between your fingers until it resembles breadcrumbs, then slowly add enough cold water to form a dough. Pop in the fridge for 10 minutes, then roll out and use as above.

Lunchtime

tortilla tarts

This is one of my 'emergency lunches', as I call them. We have these on those days where we've not got long to eat and I don't want to be faffing around with lots of pans. They might look little but they are really quite filling and they make a great addition to any picnic lunch or snacks to take in the car for a day out.

2 tortilla wraps

1 x 145g tin of tuna, drained

6 tbsp chopped tinned tomatoes or fresh tomato

2 eggs

1 handful of grated cheese (any type)

For greasing
butter or sunflower oil

1. Preheat the oven to 200°C (180°C fan). Grease a 6-hole muffin tin with a little butter or oil.

2. Place the tortilla wraps on a chopping board and cut out 6 discs of the bread, using the tuna tin as a template to cut around. Pop each disc into the holes of the muffin tin.

3. Spoon a tablespoon each of tuna and chopped tomato into each tart.

4. Whisk the eggs in a bowl and divide equally among the tarts.

5. Sprinkle some cheese over the top of each one.

6. Bake for 15 minutes.

7. Remove from the oven and serve.

8. Fine to freeze. Defrost naturally and reheat in the microwave for 30 seconds, or eat cold.

carrot and cashew pesto

Serves

4

This sweet, creamy pesto is a great option for those that love a bowl of pasta. It's full of good fats and vitamin C and is just as nice spread in sandwiches or used as a dip.

2 carrots, peeled and chopped into small chunks

1 handful of cashews

1 handful of grated Parmesan (or vegetarian hard cheese)

juice of ½ lemon

a good glug of olive oil

1. Boil the carrots in a pan of water until soft, then drain and set aside until cool.

2. Add the cooked carrots to a blender along with the cashews, Parmesan, lemon juice and olive oil, then blitz until smooth.

3. This is lovely with pasta or spread on toast or in sandwiches. Store in the fridge and eat within 2 days.

4. It is also fine to freeze. Freeze in small ice-cube trays to quickly thaw when you need a pasta sauce. It will keep for up to 6 months.

pesto
tarts

Makes

6

These would be quite at home on a silver plate being handed around at a smart drinks party...or popped in a Tupperware box and eaten at soft play.

1 handful of cherry tomatoes

2 eggs

1 handful of grated cheese (any type)

1 tsp pesto

1 sheet of ready-made shortcrust pastry

For greasing
butter or sunflower oil

1. Preheat the oven to 200°C (180°C fan). Grease a 6-hole muffin tin with a little butter or oil.

2. Chop the cherry tomatoes into quarters and place in a bowl. Add the eggs, cheese and pesto and mix until well combined.

3. Unroll the sheet of shortcrust pastry and cut out 6 discs, each about 8–10cm in diameter. Squash the discs of pastry into the holes of the prepared tin and prick the base of each one with a fork. Divide the filling mixture equally among the tart bases.

4. Bake for 30 minutes.

5. Remove from the oven, let cool slightly and serve warm.

6. Fine to freeze. Defrost naturally and reheat in the microwave for 30 seconds, or eat cold

Lunchtime

cheesy parsnip scones

Makes

6

Parsnips are such an unsung hero in my opinion! Sweet, earthy, full of vitamin C and – of crucial importance – they also happen to be BEIGE. These little scones are so easy to whip up and you'd never know there was a vegetable in sight.

1 parsnip

4 tbsp natural yoghurt

4 heaped tbsp self-raising flour

1 egg

1 handful of grated cheese (any type)

For greasing
butter or sunflower oil

1. Preheat the oven to 220°C (200°C fan). Grease a 6-hole muffin tin with a little butter or oil.

2. Grate the parsnip into a bowl, then add all the other ingredients and mix until well combined.

3. Spoon the mixture equally among the holes of the muffin tin, and squash it down with the back of a spoon.

4. Bake on the middle shelf of the oven for 30 minutes.

5. Remove from the oven and leave to cool slightly before popping them out to serve.

6. Fine to freeze and just defost naturally.

cheeseboard muffins

Makes

6

A cheeseboard is incomplete without a good dollop of chutney and few slices of crispy apple, but hang on... what about the crackers?! Well, if you imagine the wheat biscuits here are like crackers, then perhaps it makes sense. These muffins are slightly sweet, slightly salty, slightly acidic and slightly creamy, with crispy edges and soft insides. Yum!

2 apples

1 handful of grated cheese (any type)

2 eggs

1 wheat biscuit (such as Weetabix)

2 tbsp chutney of choice

For greasing
butter or sunflower oil

1. Preheat the oven to 200°C (180°C fan). Grease a 6-hole muffin tin with a little butter or oil.

2. Grate the apples into a bowl, then add the cheese and eggs, and crumble in the wheat biscuit. Mix until well combined.

3. Spoon the mixture equally among the holes of the muffin tin, then spoon a little blob of chutney on top of each one.

4. Bake for 30 minutes.

5. Remove from the oven and leave to cool slightly before popping them out to serve.

6. Fine to freeze and just defost naturally.

Lunchtime

tuna salad pinwheels

These multi-coloured pinwheels are packed with goodness. You can use fresh or frozen sweetcorn and the courgette can be swapped for grated carrot or chopped spinach.

1 x 145g tin of tuna, drained

½ courgette, grated

1 handful of sweetcorn

1 handful of grated cheese (any type)

1 sheet of ready-made puff pastry

For brushing
milk or beaten egg

1. Preheat the oven to 200°C (180°C fan). Line a baking tray with baking paper.

2. In a large bowl, mix together the tuna, grated courgette, sweetcorn and cheese.

3. Unroll the pastry sheet on the tray. Spread the tuna mixture over the whole sheet, then loosely roll it lengthways into a sausage. Slice the roll into 3cm-thick slices and arrange them flat on the baking tray (leave a good distance between each one, as they grow!). Brush each pinwheel with either milk or beaten egg.

4. Bake for 20 minutes, then remove from the oven and flip them over. Return them to the oven and bake for a further 10 minutes.

5. Remove from the oven and leave to cool slightly before serving.

6. If freezing, freeze before cooking in between sheets of greaseproof paper. Reheat from frozen as above, adding an extra 10 minutes to the cooking time.

Tip

Try not to roll the pinwheels too tightly or you will end up with raw pastry in the middle once cooked.

scrumble muffins

Makes 6

Again, we don't know why we call crumpets 'scrumbles' in our house, but we do, and these little muffins are delicious.

2 crumpets

6 cherry tomatoes

2 spring onions, finely chopped

1 handful of grated cheese (any type)

3 eggs

For greasing
butter or sunflower oil

1. Preheat the oven to 200°C (180°C fan). Grease a 6-hole muffin tin with a little butter or oil.

2. Chop the crumpets into small chunks and divide the chunks among the holes of the muffin tin.

3. Chop the tomatoes into similar-size chunks and add a few to each hole of the tin, along with a few pieces of chopped spring onion. Sprinkle a little cheese over the top of each one.

4. Beat the eggs in a jug, then pour an equal amount into each hole of the tin.

5. Bake for 25 minutes.

6. Remove from the oven and leave to cool slightly before popping the muffins out to serve.

7. Fine to freeze and just defost naturally.

spinach and halloumi mini muffins

Makes

12

Halloumi, or 'squeaky cheese' as we call it, is amazing in baking, because it goes chewy rather than melting away completely, giving these little muffins a really nice bouncy texture that doesn't crumble into nothing when you break them apart. Ideal for messy little hands! These are yummy for a lunchbox snack or a picnic. You can of course use a regular-sized muffin tin to make these – just add an extra 5 minutes to the cooking time.

1 handful of spinach

1 handful of grated halloumi cheese

1 cup (130g) self-raising flour

1 cup (250ml) milk (any type)

1 egg

For greasing
butter or sunflower oil

1. Preheat the oven to 200°C (180°C fan). Grease a 12-hole mini-muffin or cupcake tin with a little butter or oil.

2. Finely chop the spinach and place it in a bowl. Add all the other ingredients and whisk until well combined, ensuring there are no lumps.

3. Pour the mixture equally among the holes of the prepared tin.

4. Bake for 25 minutes.

5. Remove from the oven and leave to cool slightly before popping them out to serve.

6. These are fine to freeze. They are best eaten warm, so defrost naturally and reheat in the microwave for 20–30 seconds.

spiced fishcakes

Makes

8

serves 3 toddlers or 2 older children

These are so quick to whip up and are a great way to introduce a little spice to a small person's diet. Plus, if there is an avocado in the fruit bowl or fridge staring at you and threatening to turn brown at any minute, simply mash it and make fishcakes with it!

½ x 145g tin of tuna, drained

1 ripe avocado, peeled and de-stoned

2 spring onions, chopped

1 tsp garam masala or mild curry powder

1 egg

For cooking
drizzle of sunflower oil

1. Mix together all the ingredients, except the oil, in a bowl or jug until well combined, mashing the avocado well.

2. Heat a drizzle of oil in a frying pan over a medium heat. When hot, add tablespoon-sized amounts of the mixture to the pan and fry on both sides until crispy.

3. Remove each fishcake to a plate lined with kitchen paper to absorb any excess oil and that's it!

4. Serve. These are lovely with a little rice and some cress sprinkled on top.

5. Fine to freeze. Defrost naturally and then pop them in a 200°C (180°C fan) oven on a lined baking tray to reheat.

Lunchtime

carrot and sweetcorn scones

Makes
6

If, for whatever reason, you skipped a hearty breakfast, or perhaps you just have a particularly starving hungry little one, this is a great option for lunch because these are VERY filling and nutritious. These are lovely hot or cold. We like them dipped in mayonnaise or as a snack in the car or on a picnic.

1 cup (170g) couscous

1 carrot, peeled and grated

1 handful of sweetcorn

1 handful of grated cheese (any type)

3 eggs

For greasing
butter or sunflower oil

1. Preheat the oven to 200°C (180°C fan). Boil the kettle. Grease a 6-hole muffin tin with a little butter or oil.

2. Put the couscous in a bowl and add enough boiling water to just cover it. Cover with a plate and leave to steam for 5 minutes.

3. Fluff the couscous with a fork, then stir in the grated carrot (this should help it to cool down quicker).

4. Once the couscous has cooled to warm, add the other ingredients, but hold back a little of the cheese.

5. Spoon the mixture into the prepared muffin tin holes and squash down with the back of a spoon. Sprinkle the remaining cheese over the top. Bake for 30 minutes.

6. Remove from the oven and leave to cool for 15 minutes before popping them out.

7. Fine to freeze. Defrost naturally and reheat in the microwave or pop them onto a lined baking tray and into a 200°C (180°C fan) oven for 10 minutes.

Lunchtime

pear and parsnip soup

It shouldn't work, but it does! Beige, sweet, creamy and comforting – this is one you'll just have to trust me and try.

1 parsnip

knob of butter

1 low-salt chicken
stock cube

1 pear

2 tbsp double cream

1. Peel and chop the parsnip into small chunks. Add it to a saucepan with the knob of butter, and cook over a medium heat, allowing it to sweat down for 10 minutes.

2. Meanwhile, boil the kettle.

3. Measure out 500ml of boiling water, add the stock cube and mix, then pour it into the saucepan. Simmer until the parsnip is soft.

4. Using a stick blender, blitz the parsnip and stock until smooth.

5. Peel and chop the pear and add it to the saucepan. Simmer until the pear turns soft.

6. Once again, blitz until smooth.

7. Stir in the double cream and that's it. It's ready to serve.

Tip

Swirl in some olive oil or extra cream and sprinkle with black pepper for serving to grown-ups.

cheese and onion pinwheels

Serves

4

Cheese and onion pastries don't exactly conjure up the idea of a healthy lunch, do they? However, spring onions are rich in vitamins and cheese is full of good fats and calcium – even the feistiest little veg-phobe would struggle to say no to them. Especially after they've smelt them come fresh out of the oven!

1 spring onion

1 sheet of ready-made puff pastry

1 tbsp cream cheese

a sprinkling of grated cheese (any type)

For brushing
milk or beaten egg

1. Preheat the oven to 200°C (180°C fan). Line a baking tray with baking paper.

2. Slice the spring onion into little chunks.

3. Unroll the pastry sheet and thinly spread the cream cheese over the whole sheet. Sprinkle over the spring onion and grated cheese, then loosely roll it up lengthways into a sausage (not too tight or you'll have raw pastry). Slice into 3cm-thick slices and pop them on the baking tray, spaced well apart. Brush with either milk or beaten egg.

4. Bake for 25 minutes.

5. Remove from the oven and serve.

If you want to freeze these, freeze the raw pinwheels and bake from frozen by adding an extra 5 minutes onto the cooking time.

broccoli and cheddar bites

Serves
2

I think this might be the most popular recipe I've ever shared online and the reason for it is simple – these are super quick and easy. I often make them if I've got some tired-looking broccoli in the fridge. They are great finger food. Just as tasty cold as they are hot and not (too) messy, these are really yummy dipped in Greek yoghurt or some mayo.

1 cup (170g) couscous

1 head of broccoli

2 eggs

1 handful of grated
Cheddar cheese

For cooking
drizzle of sunflower oil

1. Boil the kettle.

2. Put the couscous in a bowl and add enough boiling water to just cover it. Cover with a plate and leave to steam for about 5 minutes.

3. Meanwhile, chop the broccoli into very small chunks.

4. When the couscous is ready, add the broccoli and mix until well combined. Leave to cool slightly.

5. When cool, add the eggs and grated cheese.

6. Heat a drizzle of oil in a frying pan over a medium heat. When hot, add tablespoon-sized amounts of the mixture and fry until golden and crispy on both sides, squashing them down with the back of a spatula once you've cooked the first side.

7. Remove each bite to a plate lined with kitchen paper to absorb any excess oil and that's it. Serve immediately.

8. Fine to freeze. Defrost naturally and reheat in the microwave for 30 seconds, or eat cold.

brocciflower cheese

Serves

1

When we have Sunday lunch, I often do four or five simple vegetable side dishes (usually just steamed with a little butter and pepper), but if your little one is anything like Harry was, the meat and potatoes disappear quicker than you can say 'bon appetit', leaving a pile of abandoned veggies, swimming in gravy and feeling sorry for themselves. This is a good alternative for them – or, indeed, for the whole family!

1 handful of broccoli florets

1 handful of cauliflower florets

1 tbsp natural yoghurt

1 handful of grated cheese (any type)

1. Preheat the oven to 220°C (200°C fan).

2. Blitz the broccoli and cauliflower in a blender until it has broken down into tiny chunks. Add the yoghurt and cheese, and blitz again to combine.

3. Pour the mixture into an ovenproof dish.

4. Bake for 40 minutes.

5. Serve!

no-blend pea and potato soup

Serves

2

I love soup but often I can't be bothered with all the blitzing and process involved, so this is a great 'throw it all together' recipe for a hearty bowl of hot soup. This is really nice with a sprinkling of grated cheese across the top. I like it with some chilli flakes and black pepper, too.

1 white potato

½ x 300g tin of mushy peas

½ low- or zero-salt vegetable stock cube

drizzle of double cream (optional)

1. Boil the kettle.

2. Peel and chop the potato into small chunks. Add it to a saucepan, cover with boiling water and boil until soft.

3. Drain and mash the potato and return it to the saucepan along with the mushy peas, stock cube and a cupful (250ml) of boiling water. Bring to a simmer, then use a whisk to break down the potato.

4. That's it – it's ready to serve! You can add a drop of cream too (and some chilli flakes for the grown-ups), if you wish.

5. Fine to freeze. Defrost naturally and reheat as needed.

cheesy leek puffs

These are a 'must try', even if they don't sound very exciting. Flaky pastry, sweet leeks and creamy cheese! The first time I made these, I took one through for Tom to try and he said it was his favourite of all my recipes. I suppose this is all to say, I fully recommend making enough of these for you to have one of your own, because they are certainly 'adult-friendly'.

1 leek, chopped

1 tbsp cream cheese

1 handful of grated cheese (any type)

1 sheet of puff pastry

For brushing
milk or beaten egg

1. Place the leek in a small pan of water and boil until soft. Drain and set aside in a bowl until cool.

2. Meanwhile, preheat the oven to 200°C (180°C fan). Line a baking tray with baking paper.

3. When the leek is cool, mix in the cream cheese and grated cheese.

4. Unroll the puff pastry sheet straight from the fridge and slice it widthways into 4 rectangles.

5. Spoon the leek and cheese mixture equally between the rectangles, arranging it on just one side of each rectangle and leaving a 1–2cm border around the edges.

6. Fold over the empty side of the pastry rectangles to cover the filling and use a fork to seal the three open sides. Pierce the top of each parcel with a sharp knife.

7. Pop them on the baking tray and brush with either milk or beaten egg, then bake for 30 minutes.

8. Serve warm but not too hot. Split them in half to let the steam out before giving to a toddler!

Lunchtime

salmon and courgette fritters

Makes

8

Serves

2

Fritters make a great quick meal or snack and the flavour options are quite literally endless. They are also so easy to make. These are lovely served with a small salad of chopped cucumber drizzled with a little sesame oil and with some white sesame seeds sprinkled on top.

1 x 213g tin of skinless and boneless salmon

1 courgette, grated

2 eggs

4 heaped tbsp self-raising flour

1 tsp reduced-salt soy sauce (see Tip)

For cooking
drizzle of sunflower oil

1. Combine all the ingredients, except the oil, in a bowl and mix thoroughly.

2. Heat a drizzle of oil in a frying pan over a medium heat. Dollop tablespoon-sized blobs of the mixture into the hot pan and fry until golden brown on both sides. Remove from the pan with a slotted spoon and pat dry with kitchen paper.

3. We like these dipped in ketchup or mayo, or with a salad, as mentioned above.

4. They will keep for up to 48 hours in a sealed container in the fridge. They are also fine to freeze. Defrost naturally and reheat in the microwave or bake on a lined baking tray in a 200°C (180°C fan) oven for 10 minutes.

Tip

If soy sauce is an allergen for your child, cream cheese makes a good alternative here.

Lunchtime

Four

Sweet Snacks

Sweet Snacks

If your little ones are still having a post-lunch nap, then you'll identify with the need for something a little sweet in the middle of the afternoon to boost their energy levels. Equally, if you are running low on entertainment ideas for the rest of the day, lots of these are fun and easy enough that you can make them together. I always think it's great to get little ones helping in the kitchen from a young age if you can handle the mess and bold execution on their part. But if it's the post-nursery or school munchies you need to curb, then look no further!

lemon drizzle (ish)

Serves

4–6

Do you like lemon drizzle cake? Silly question, because of course you do. However, it's sadly full of sugar and it's difficult to explain to hungry little ones why they can't share your slice of cake (and obviously no one likes sharing a slice of cake in the first place). So, here is a recipe for a low-sugar version that you can all enjoy together. I use sunflower oil to make this, but you can use vegetable or coconut oil instead.

1 lemon

6 tbsp sunflower, vegetable or coconut oil

3 eggs

1 cup (130g) self-raising flour

2 tbsp lemon curd

1. Preheat the oven to 200°C (180°C fan). Line a 22 x 10 x 6cm loaf tin with baking paper.

2. Zest the lemon and place the zest in a mixing bowl. Add the oil, eggs, flour, 1 tablespoon of the lemon curd and the juice of half of the lemon. Mix thoroughly, ensuring there are no lumps.

3. Pour the batter into the prepared tin. Bake for 30 minutes (or until a skewer inserted into the loaf comes out clean).

4. Remove from the oven and use a fork or skewer to prick lots of holes across the top of the loaf.

5. In a small bowl, combine the juice of the other half of the lemon with the remaining tablespoon of lemon curd, mixing together to form a syrup.

6. Remove the cake from the tin and, while it is still warm, drizzle over the lemon syrup.

7. Leave it to rest until it is nearly cool before slicing.

8. Fine to freeze. Defrost naturally before serving.

Sweet Snacks

cinnamon pear biscuits

Makes 6

It's always the pears that seem to get forgotten about in our fruit bowl, then you have to almost decant them into the food bin with a spoon because they've turned to slush. Well, here is a great recipe to use up exactly those sorts of pears. If you can peel them, great, if you can't because they're too mushy – just mash them whole and pick out the stalk and pips to make the batter and they'll be just as good.

2 very ripe pears

1 cup (100g) porridge oats

2 tbsp milk (any type – works particularly well with oat milk)

1 tsp ground cinnamon

1. Preheat the oven to 200°C (180°C fan). Line a baking tray with baking paper.

2. Peel and core the pears, then mash them in a bowl.

3. Add the other ingredients and mix until well combined.

4. Split the dough into 6 equal pieces, then roll each one into a biscuit-shaped patty. Pop them on the lined baking tray, spaced well apart.

5. Bake for 15 minutes.

6. Remove them from the oven and leave until just about cool before popping them off the tray.

7. That's it. These are lovely dipped in warm milk.

8. Fine to freeze for up to 6 months. Just freeze the cooked biscuits on the lined tray. Defrost naturally and either eat them cold or pop them in a 200°C (180°C fan) oven (still on the lined tray) for 10 minutes to reheat.

blackberry and lemon flapjack cookies

Makes

6

Sticky, sweet, slightly acidic and very purple – these beauties look and taste amazing.

1 cup (100g) porridge oats

3 tbsp (50ml) milk (any type)

1 tbsp peanut butter (any type)

2 tbsp lemon curd

1 handful of blackberries

1. Preheat the oven to 200°C (180°C fan). Line a baking tray with baking paper.

2. Gently mix all the ingredients together in a bowl until well combined, taking care not to crush the blackberries too much. Spoon tablespoon-sized amounts onto the prepared tray, leaving gaps between them.

3. Bake for 30 minutes.

4. Remove from the oven and leave to cool before serving.

5. Fine to freeze. Defrost naturally and reheat in the microwave for 20 seconds, or eat cold.

Tip

The blackberries can be swapped for any other kind of berries, fresh or frozen.

banana bread

The riper the bananas, the more delicious this is! With just three ingredients and absolutely no added sugar, this is a great alternative to banana bread as we know it, for little ones and babies. It doesn't crumble like traditional cake so it's the perfect texture to hold and is certainly simple enough to make together.

3 ripe bananas

4 wheat biscuits
(such as Weetabix)

4 eggs

1. Preheat the oven to 200°C (180°C fan). Line a 22 x 10 x 6cm loaf tin with baking paper.

2. Mash 2 of the bananas in a bowl, then crumble in the wheat biscuits. Add the eggs and mix together until well combined.

3. Pour the mixture into the prepared tin. Slice the final banana lengthways and place it on top of the mixture.

4. Bake for 25 minutes, or until a skewer inserted into the loaf comes out clean (it may need another 5 minutes).

5. Remove from the oven and leave to cool before slicing.

6. If freezing, slice and freeze individual slices between sheets of baking paper. Defrost naturally and pop in the microwave for 20 seconds, or eat cold.

strawberry and vanilla loaf cake

Serves
4

This is so moist and naturally sweet, it's a perfect loaf to make and enjoy on a warm summer's day after a danger nap to see you through until tea!

150g (or 2 handfuls) strawberries, chopped, plus extra to decorate (optional)

2 tbsp coconut oil, softened

1 cup (130g) self-raising flour

2 tbsp vanilla extract

2 eggs

1. Preheat the oven to 200°C (180°C fan). Line a 27.5 x 12 x 6cm loaf tin with baking paper.

2. Combine all the ingredients in a bowl, beating the mixture together to get rid of any lumps of flour.

3. Pour the mixture into the prepared tin. If you like, you can chop a few strawberries lengthways and arrange them on top of the batter, to decorate.

4. Bake for 20 minutes.

5. Remove from the oven and leave to cool before popping it out and slicing it.

6. Fine to freeze. Defrost naturally before serving.

healthy chocolate mini pancakes

Serves

1

The words 'healthy' and 'chocolate' are not usually found together in a sentence but these are just that.

1 banana

1 tsp cocoa powder

3 tbsp porridge oats

1 tbsp smooth peanut butter

1 egg

For cooking
drizzle of sunflower oil

1. Mash the banana in a bowl, then add all the other ingredients, except the oil, and mix together until there are no lumps.

2. Heat a drizzle of oil in a frying pan over a medium heat. Add tablespoon-sized amounts of the mixture to the pan and fry for about 3 minutes on each side until firm.

3. Serve immediately. We like them drizzled with extra peanut butter and some fresh berries.

4. Fine to freeze. To cook from frozen, allow the pancakes to defrost naturally, then reheat in the microwave or in a dry frying pan.

peach and apricot flapjacks

Makes

12

Stone fruits are great for baking, as they become sticky and sweeter when cooked. These are ideal for picnic weather or as a comforting warm snack on a cold afternoon. They also make a great filling breakfast!

2 cups (200g) porridge oats

generous ½ cup (100ml) milk (any type)

1 banana, mashed

2 peaches, chopped into small chunks

1 tbsp apricot jam

1. Preheat the oven to 200°C (180°C fan). Line an ovenproof dish (about 25 x 16.5 x 3.5cm) with baking paper.

2. Combine all the ingredients in a bowl until well mixed.

3. Tip the mixture into the prepared dish and squash it level with the back of a spoon.

4. Bake for 30 minutes.

5. Remove and leave to cool before slicing into rectangles.

6. Fine to freeze. Defrost naturally before serving.

Sweet Snacks

yoghurty apple pancakes

Makes
5–6

These creamy, sweet pancakes are so easy to make and the apple sauce or purée can be swapped for any flavour fruit pouch or homemade fruit compôte.

1 cup (100g) porridge oats

4 tbsp yoghurt (any type)

2 tbsp apple sauce

1 egg

1 tbsp chia seeds

For cooking
sunflower oil or butter

1. If you want the pancakes to be smooth, blitz the oats into a flour in a food processor, but it's up to you.

2. Place the oats in a bowl, add the yoghurt, apple sauce, egg and chia seeds, and mix until well combined.

3. Heat a little oil or butter in a frying pan over a medium heat. Ladle the mixture into the pan in 5–6 spoonfuls and fry on both sides until golden.

4. Serve immediately!

blueberry yoghurt muffins

Makes 6

Harry knows this recipe off by heart and can make these without any help from me whatsoever. The texture is chewy rather than crumbly so they are certainly less messy than a traditional muffin, which makes them ideal for little ones.

1 handful of blueberries

2 tbsp full-fat natural yoghurt

4 tbsp self-raising flour

1 tbsp jam (any flavour)

1 egg

For greasing
butter or sunflower oil

1. Preheat the oven to 200°C (180°C fan). Grease a 6-hole muffin tin with a little butter or oil (don't use paper cases).

2. Mix all the ingredients together in a bowl, beating all the lumps out.

3. Spoon the mixture equally between the holes of the prepared tin.

4. Bake for 25 minutes.

5. Remove from the oven and leave to cool before serving.

6. Fine to freeze. Defrost naturally before serving.

fruity muffins

Makes

6

No sugar, no dairy and full of fruit – these might sound like they'd taste a little bland but they are anything but. We're so accustomed to the flavour of highly sugary food but our little ones' palates aren't yet, so these guilt-free muffins can be enjoyed at any time of day. I usually serve them to Harry as an after-school or nursery snack.

1 ripe banana

1 handful of chopped strawberries

1 handful of blueberries

1 egg

1 cup (130g) self-raising flour

For greasing
butter or sunflower oil

1. Preheat the oven to 200°C (180°C fan). Grease a 6-hole muffin tin or silicone cases with a little butter or oil.

2. Mash the banana in a bowl, then add the other ingredients and mix until well combined.

3. Spoon the mixture into the holes of the prepared tin.

4. Bake for 25 minutes.

5. Remove from the oven and leave them to cool before popping them out to serve.

6. Fine to freeze. Defrost naturally before serving.

spiced apple bars

Makes

12

If you want your home to smell like a Danish bakery in the afternoon then I highly recommend these! They really do smell amazing and will certainly stave off any afternoon munchies.

2 cups (200g) porridge oats

generous ⅓ cup (100ml) milk

2 apples, grated with the skins on

1 banana

1 tbsp mixed spice

For decorating
extra apple, thinly sliced and cut into shapes of your choosing (optional)

1. Preheat the oven to 200°C (180°C fan). Line a baking tin (about 25 x 16.5 x 3.5cm) with baking paper.

2. Combine all the ingredients in a bowl until well combined.

3. Spoon the mixture into the prepared tin and squash it down with the back of a spoon. If you like, you can add some apple slices or shapes to the top of each one to decorate.

4. Bake for 30 minutes.

5. Remove from the oven and leave to cool before slicing into squares.

6. Fine to freeze. Defrost naturally before serving.

raspberry yoghurt flatbreads

Serves

1

Raspberries go squishy very quickly and this is a great way to use them up. These little pink breads are super-easy to make – you could easily make them together.

4 tbsp (30g) self-raising flour, or as needed, plus extra for dusting

2 heaped tbsp (30g) raspberry yoghurt, or as needed

For cooking
drizzle of sunflower oil

To serve
1 handful of fresh raspberries

1 tsp raspberry yoghurt

1. Combine the flour and yoghurt in a bowl to form a dough. If the dough is too wet, add a little extra flour; too crumbly, add a little more yoghurt.

2. Turn the dough out onto a floured board and roll it out into 2 rough circles.

3. Heat a drizzle of oil in a frying pan over a medium heat. Add the breads to the pan and cook until bubbles start to appear, then use tongs to flip the breads over and cook the other sides.

4. Pop the breads onto a plate.

5. Mash the raspberries with the teaspoon of raspberry yoghurt and spoon the mixture on top of the flatbreads.

6. Serve.

7. The breads are fine to freeze for up to 6 months. Defrost naturally, then reheat in the microwave for 20 seconds.

Sweet Snacks

strawberry oatcakes

Makes

6

Pretty as a picture and packed full of vitamins, these will look store-bought but are surprisingly simple.

1 cup (100g) porridge oats

3 tbsp (50ml) milk

1 banana

3 handfuls of chopped strawberries, plus extra to decorate

1 tbsp strawberry jam

1. Preheat the oven to 200°C (180°C fan). Grease a 6-hole muffin tin with a little oil or butter.

2. Combine all the ingredients in a bowl. Mix until well combined, thoroughly mashing the banana and strawberries.

3. Spoon the mixture into the holes of the prepared tin and use the back of a spoon to push it down. Add some extra chopped strawberries to the top of each one to decorate.

4. Bake for 30 minutes.

5. Remove from the oven and leave them to cool before popping them out to serve.

6. Fine to freeze. Defrost naturally before serving.

warm spiced pear smoothie

Serves

1

This is perfect for a chilly early morning or for a treat after a cold trip to the park. If you have any leftovers, pour the mixture into ice-lolly moulds and they make the most delicious ice pops for a warmer day. It tastes as good as it sounds!

½ cup (125ml) milk (any type)

½ x 400g tin of pears, plus a good glug of the syrup from the tin

a pinch of ground nutmeg

a pinch of ground cinnamon

1. Add everything to a blender and blitz until smooth.

2. Pour the smoothie into a microwaveable cup and microwave for 20 seconds (or until warm).

3. Serve immediately.

Five

Dinners

Dinners

Whether you eat together as a family every evening or not,
all of these recipes can be enjoyed by adults and children alike.
Dinner is Harry's favourite meal of the day and we usually sit at the
table with him (even if we aren't eating together) to chat about his
day. It's often a complicated thread with lots of tangents, repetition,
random giggling and unrelated questions, but the food itself need
not be complex. Lots of these recipes involve one pan, tray or dish
and are packed with plenty of veggies to keep your little ones full
and hopefully ensure a good night's sleep...

courgette and chorizo pasta

Serves **2**

This is a great family dish and certainly not lacking in flavour! Chorizo can obviously be quite salty and quite hard for little teeth to break down – if your little one is under one, you can chop the chorizo into big chunks and remove the slices before serving, because they'll still get that delicious smoky flavour as part of their dinner and it's good to get them used to strong flavours from a young age. Harry loves chorizo, which is just as well because we all do, so this is a firm family favourite! You can double up quantities to feed more easily.

½ courgette

1 cup (about 80g) small pasta shapes of choice (such as ditalini or pasta stars)

1 small handful of finely diced chorizo

1 tbsp cream cheese

1 lemon wedge

For cooking
sunflower oil or butter

1. Grate the courgette and set aside.

2. Cook the pasta according to the packet instructions, then drain and set aside.

3. Heat a little oil or butter in a frying pan over a medium heat. Fry the chorizo until crispy, then add the grated courgette and fry for a few minutes. Add the cooked pasta and cream cheese, then squeeze in the juice of the lemon wedge and mix until well combined.

4. Serve immediately.

5. I don't advise freezing this once the pasta has been combined with the sauce.

Dinners

sausage, apple and mango loaf

Serves

4

Meatloaf is a lovely dish to enjoy together and this version is slightly sweet, contains no salt and is very filling, so a little goes a long way. We usually have this with creamy mashed potatoes and some greens and everyone enjoys it. It is also delicious thinly sliced in a sandwich and perfect for picnics.

500g lean pork mince

1 cup (100g) porridge oats

2 apples, grated

2 eggs

2 tbsp mango chutney, plus extra for glazing

1. Preheat the oven to 200°C (180°C fan). Line a 22 x 10 x 6cm loaf tin with baking paper.

2. Mix together all the ingredients in a bowl until well combined.

3. Pour the mixture into the prepared tin and level the surface with the back of a spoon.

4. Bake for 45 minutes.

5. Remove from the oven and poke some holes in the top with a fork. Brush a little extra mango chutney over the surface of the loaf and set aside until nearly cool.

6. Slice and serve.

7. If freezing, slice and freeze slices between sheets of greaseproof paper. Defrost naturally and reheat in the oven at 200°C (180°C fan) for 15 minutes.

Dinners

margherita flatbread

Makes

1

A very quick dinner is sometimes just what the doctor ordered and this recipe is exactly that. Most children enjoy pizza and this rustic homemade version is a brilliant alternative. My Harry wouldn't touch basil leaves, but for the fully authentic margherita experience, feel free to add a few leaves on top to serve.

6 tbsp (50g) self-raising flour, or as needed, plus extra for dusting

¼ cup (50g) natural yoghurt, or as needed

1 tbsp tomato purée

1 handful of grated mozzarella cheese

For cooking
drizzle of sunflower oil

1. Preheat the oven to 200°C (180°C fan).

2. Combine the flour and yoghurt in a bowl to form a dough. If it is too wet, add a little extra flour; too dry, add a little more yoghurt.

3. Roll the dough out on a floured surface into a rough circle.

4. Heat a drizzle of oil in a frying pan over a medium heat. Add the dough circle and fry on side one until bubbles start to appear, then use tongs to flip it over and crisp up the other side. This should take about 5 minutes in total.

5. Remove the flatbread from the pan, spread the tomato purée over one side and sprinkle the mozzarella on top. Place on a baking tray lined with baking paper.

6. Bake for 5 minutes, then serve.

Flatbreads are fine to freeze, so I often batch make them, then freeze them between layers of baking paper. I add the toppings after taking them out of the freezer and bake from frozen (an extra 2–3 minutes is required).

Dinners

avocado and prawn pasta

This is a lovely dish for the whole family to enjoy together. Mashed avocado is an amazing thing, add some prawns or even some sweet flaked salmon and throw it in with pasta and you've got a super healthy dinner, packed with goodness.

1 cup (about 80g) pasta of choice

1 handful of raw prawns

1 avocado, peeled and de-stoned

1 handful of grated Parmesan

1 lemon wedge

1. Cook the pasta in a pan of boiling water according to the packet instructions. About 5 minutes before the pasta has finished cooking, add the prawns to the pan to cook with the pasta.

2. Mash the avocado in a bowl, then add the Parmesan and squeeze in the juice of the lemon wedge.

3. When the pasta and prawns are cooked (the prawns should be pink and will slice in one go if you use a knife to cut one open), drain, then combine them with the avocado sauce.

4. Serve immediately.

Tip

This is easy to bulk out with extra pasta, another avocado and a few extra prawns to feed the whole family.

tuna leeky pasta

This is something my mum used to make for me as a child and I still love it now. Leeks are a great vegetable for picky eaters because, unlike a lot of other green vegetables, which retain their essential bitterness, leeks become sweet!

1 handful of pasta of choice

1 handful of chopped leek

1 x 145g tin of tuna, drained

2 tbsp cream cheese

1. Cook the pasta according to the packet instructions.

2. Halfway through the pasta cooking, add the leek to the boiling pasta pan.

3. When the pasta is cooked, drain and return the pasta and leek to the pan. Add the tuna and cream cheese and mix thoroughly.

4. Serve immediately.

Dinners

avocado (aka thursday) pasta

Let me explain. I buy 'ripen-at-home' avocados because they are considerably cheaper and I usually do my food shop on a Friday morning. This means that by Thursday we are a) running low on fresh ingredients and b) my avocados are ready to eat! This dish is incredibly quick and filling and you could even get your little minion(s) to make the sauce themselves, because mashing avocados is quite a nice thing to do. Either way, I always wish I'd made more of this whenever I make it because it's proper comfort food and I secretly hope Harry will leave a little so I can finish it. Sadly he never does...

1 handful of pasta of choice

2 avocados, peeled and de-stoned

1 tbsp cream cheese

1 lemon wedge

1 handful of finely grated cheese (any type)

1. Cook the pasta according to the packet instructions.

2. In a large mixing bowl, mash the avocados with the cream cheese, juice of the lemon wedge and the grated cheese until well combined and creamy.

3. When the pasta is cooked, drain and mix with the avocado sauce.

4. It's ready to serve. You can have this hot or cold – it's great both ways.

bobble pie

Serves

2

Named by Harry, you won't be surprised to hear. This is what I call an 'emergency dinner', because you might find you refer to this recipe when you're due a food shop the following day and there's almost nothing in the house. Easy, filling and fuss-free.

1 white potato, peeled and chopped

½ x 400g tin of baked beans

1 tbsp frozen peas

1 tbsp frozen sweetcorn

1 handful of grated cheese (any type)

1. Preheat the oven to 200°C (180°C fan).

2. Cook the potato in a pan of boiling water until soft, then drain and mash.

3. In a small ovenproof dish, combine the baked beans, peas and sweetcorn. Mix together, then spoon over the mashed potato and sprinkle over the cheese.

4. Bake for 20 minutes.

5. Remove from the oven and serve.

6. This is fine to freeze. It can be cooked straight from frozen in a 200°C (180°C fan) oven for 20 minutes, or until piping hot.

172

Dinners

my first curry

When you think of curry, you probably imagine you've got to whizz to the supermarket to buy 17 different spices you'll never use again and that's if you actually find the ones you went for in the first place. Well, this recipe calls for just one and it's probably the one you've already got! It's great to expose little ones to spices from an early age because spice doesn't necessarily mean 'spicy' and if you're hoping to raise an adventurous little foodie, this is a great place to start. Exposure is key. This recipe is great for smuggling in a few extra veggies you have lying around and takes about 15 minutes from start to finish.

1 handful of chopped chicken breast (or Quorn, tofu or prawns)

1 tsp mild curry powder

1 tbsp tomato purée

½ x 400g tin of full-fat coconut milk

cooked rice, to serve (optional)

For cooking
drizzle of sunflower oil

1. Place the chicken (or other main ingredient) in a saucepan along with the curry powder and oil and stir over a medium heat. When the chicken (or other main ingredient) is thoroughly coated in the curry powder and starting to catch at the bottom of the pan, add the tomato purée and cook for 1 minute.

2. Add the coconut milk and simmer for about 10 minutes, stirring occasionally.

3. That's it! Serve, ideally spooned over hot rice.

Dinners

bolognese pinwheels

Spag Bol is an absolute staple in our house. When all else failed, I could guarantee that Harry would eat it. However, it usually involved an industrial clean up afterwards: stain-remover, a mop, maybe having to repaint the walls, and that's not including the orange child needing a bath! This method of delivery is considerably less messy and easier for small hands that may or may not have got the hang of cutlery yet.

500g minced beef

3 carrots, grated

2 handfuls of chopped cherry tomatoes

1 sheet of puff pastry

2 handfuls of grated cheese (any type)

Additional

sunflower oil or butter, for cooking

250ml (1 cup) freshly boiled water

salt and pepper (optional)

milk or beaten egg, for brushing

1. Heat a little oil or butter in a pan over a medium heat, add the mince and cook until browned. Add the carrots, tomatoes and boiling water and simmer for 20 minutes, or until all the water has evaporated, stirring occasionally. Season to taste (if you wish), then leave to cool.

2. Preheat the oven to 200°C (180°C fan). Line a baking tray with baking paper.

3. Unroll the pastry and spoon the cooled sauce over the whole sheet. Sprinkle over the cheese (or see Tip below). Roll up the pastry to form a sausage (not too tightly). Chop the sausage into discs, each about 2.5cm thick, and lay them flat on the prepared baking tray.

4. Brush with either milk or beaten egg. Bake for 25 minutes.

5. Remove from the oven and they're ready to serve.

6. Fine to freeze. Defrost naturally and then pop them in a 200°C (180°C fan) oven on a lined baking tray to reheat.

Tip *If you like, you can save the cheese for sprinkling on top of the pinwheels just before baking.*

Dinners

quick satay

Serves
1

Don't ignore this recipe because you don't believe it really is 'quick'. I've rustled this one up in just five minutes once I've found the tin opener! You can add whatever quick-cooking veg you have around (sweetcorn, spring onion, green beans, etc.) and it's a great recipe for those evenings when you need to get something on the table as quickly as you can.

2 tbsp smooth peanut butter

1 tsp low-salt soy sauce

½ x 400g tin of full-fat coconut milk

1 chicken breast, chopped

½ red pepper, chopped

For cooking
drizzle of sunflower oil

1. Mix together the peanut butter, soy sauce and coconut milk to make the sauce.

2. Heat the oil in a frying pan over a medium heat, add the chicken and fry until golden brown on all sides. Add the pepper and pour over the sauce, then simmer until the pepper has softened. That's it!

3. Serve hot.

campfire stew with baked sweet potatoes

Serves

1–2

This is a great dish for all the family and only requires the use of one saucepan so there's minimal washing up.

1-2 sweet potatoes

1 rasher of bacon, chopped

½ red pepper, chopped

½ x 400g tin of chopped tomatoes

½ x 400g tin of baked beans

For cooking
drizzle of sunflower oil

1. Preheat the oven to 200°C (180°C fan).

2. Bake the sweet potato/es for 30 minutes.

3. Meanwhile, heat a tiny drizzle of oil in a saucepan that has a lid over a medium heat, then add the bacon and fry for a couple of minutes. When the bacon is starting to crisp up, add the pepper and fry for 1 minute, then add the tomatoes and beans. Mix well and reduce the heat down to low, then place the lid on the pan and leave it to simmer for 15 minutes.

4. Slice the baked potato/es in half and spoon the campfire stew over the top to serve.

tomato dal

I often make this when Harry has been a little under the weather, because it's full of vitamin C and very comforting. A warm bowl of lentils is good for the soul and leftovers can be used as the base for a soup or simply served as a warm dip with some bread.

2 cups (500ml) cold water

1 cup (180g) red lentils

1 tbsp garlic paste
(or 3 finely chopped
garlic cloves)

2 handfuls of cherry
tomatoes

½ low-salt vegetable
stock cube

1. Place all the ingredients in a saucepan and bring to a simmer over a medium heat. Cook for 20 minutes, stirring occasionally.

2. That really is it!

3. This is lovely served with a hunk of bread for dipping and can be eaten like soup with a spoon.

4. Fine to freeze for up to 6 months. Defrost naturally, then reheat in a saucepan to serve.

Dinners

veggie lasagne

Lasagne is a staple in lots of houses but it can be a bit of a faff whipping up a béchamel and a flavoursome Bolognese sauce (without adding mounds of salt), then layering it, etc. This version, however, is very simple and considerably healthier. We often have this as a midweek meal served with chips and salad. Use a loaf tin to make this if you have one, as lasagne sheets fit perfectly inside it and it saves you cutting them to size or layering too many over each other and running the risk of uncooked, chewy pasta.

1 x 100g bag of spinach

1 x 250g tub of ricotta

4 lasagne sheets

⅔ x 400g tin of chopped tomatoes

1 handful of grated cheese (any type)

1. Preheat the oven to 200°C (180°C fan).

2. Place the spinach in a microwaveable bowl with 2 tablespoons of cold water. Cook on high for 1 minute until soft, then drain.

3. Add the ricotta to the spinach and mix thoroughly.

4. Layer up the lasagne in a 2lb loaf tin: first, place a layer of pasta sheets, followed by a layer of the spinach mixture, then add a few tablespoons of chopped tomatoes. Repeat until you have used up all your ingredients. Top with the grated cheese.

5. Bake for 40 minutes. Remove from the oven and set aside to firm up for 10 minutes, then slice and serve.

You can batch make this ahead of time and freeze before cooking. To cook from frozen, add an extra 15 minutes to the cooking time. I don't recommend freezing this once cooked. You can, of course, reheat it from chilled and serve it again within 48 hours if you keep it in the fridge.

Dinners

aubergine risotto

Vegetables come in every colour imaginable but the inside of the humble aubergine is beige! When Harry was going through his very worst vegetable aversions, this was my go-to recipe because it looks like a bowl of creamy, cheesy rice, which he'd happily shovel in and be none-the-wiser. Your secret is safe with me! This is particularly lovely served with a squeeze of lemon juice at the end, too.

1 aubergine

½ low-salt vegetable stock cube

1 cup (190g) arborio or other risotto rice

1 tbsp cream cheese

2 tbsp grated Parmesan or vegetarian hard cheese

For cooking
knob of butter or drizzle of sunflower oil

To serve (optional)
lemon wedges

a few sprigs of parsley, chopped

1. Preheat the oven to 220°C (200°C fan).

2. Halve the aubergine and place it, cut-sides up, on a baking tray. Bake for 30 minutes.

3. Remove the aubergine from the oven and scoop the flesh out of the skins into a bowl.

4. Combine the stock cube half with 1 cup (250ml) boiling water and set aside.

5. Place the rice in a saucepan along with the butter (or oil, if needed) and set over a low heat. When you can smell toasted rice and hear a little fizzing noise, add the stock little by little, stirring regularly to stop the rice from sticking to the pan. When you can feel the rice is starting to soften, add the aubergine pulp. When the rice is completely soft (after about 20 minutes), add the cream cheese and Parmesan, then turn off the heat and stir to let out the steam.

6. Just before serving, squeeze in the lemon juice and add a sprig of parsley, if using.

7. This doesn't freeze and I don't recommend reheating it, unless you have cooled it immediately after cooking and reheat to piping hot all the way through before serving.

mustardy gnocci bake

This is a great dinner when you just want to bung something in the oven and have a few minutes to yourself (or more likely wrestle a crayon off your little one who seems adamant on redecorating the lounge while your back is turned). Wholegrain mustard is quite a strong flavour, but the amount required is very tiny and it's another great taste to expose little ones to. It's a great dish for all the family and is very nice with some fried bacon lardons added to it.

1 packet of gnocchi

1 handful of peas (fresh or frozen)

⅔ cup (150ml) double cream

1 tsp wholegrain mustard

1 handful of grated cheese (any type)

1. Preheat the oven to 200°C (180°C fan).

2. Pour the gnocchi into an ovenproof dish. Sprinkle over the peas, tip in the cream and add the mustard. Mix with a spoon until the mustard and cream are well combined. Sprinkle over the cheese.

3. Bake for 25 minutes.

4. Remove and leave to cool slightly before serving.

5. This is fine to freeze, but I'd be amazed if you have any leftovers! Defrost naturally and then reheat either in the microwave for 30 seconds or pop in a 200°C (180°C fan) oven for 15 minutes.

thai sweet potato curry

Creamy, sweet and fragrant – at first glance you might not believe this could taste, look or smell so good with so few ingredients, but please don't be cynical – it's a real crowd-pleaser and can have lots of other veg or protein added to it.

1 sweet potato

1 tsp Thai 7-spice powder

1 handful of cherry tomatoes, chopped

½ x 400g tin of coconut milk

For cooking
glug of sunflower oil

1. Peel and chop the sweet potato, then add it to a saucepan with a glug of oil and set over a medium heat.

2. After a couple of minutes, add the Thai 7-spice powder and stir until the sweet potato is fully coated.

3. Add the tomatoes and the coconut milk, and leave to simmer for 15 minutes, or until the sweet potato is soft.

4. Serve.

Dinners

secret mac and cheese (secretly packed with veg)

Another beige wonder of the universe is cauliflower! Creamy sweet cauliflower mixed with pasta and cheese, then baked to give it a crispy topping... I hope I'm selling it to you because this healthy version of a traditional mac and cheese makes a delicious dinner for the entire family.

1 small white onion, chopped

½ cauliflower, chopped

generous ⅓ cup (100ml) double cream

2 handfuls of grated cheese (any type)

1 handful of macaroni pasta

For cooking
sunflower oil or butter

1. Preheat the oven to 220°C (200°C fan).

2. Heat a little oil or butter in a saucepan that has a lid over a low heat. Add the onion and sweat until translucent, then add the cauliflower and ½ cup (125ml) boiling water. Pop the lid on the pan and leave it to steam for 10 minutes (check from time to time, to make sure it doesn't dry out and start to catch on the bottom of the pan).

3. Drain the onion and cauliflower and add to a blender or food processor, along with the cream and 1½ handfuls of the cheese. Blitz until completely smooth, adding a little sunflower oil to help it along, if needed.

4. In another pan, cook the pasta according to the packet instructions.

5. Drain the pasta, then combine it with the sauce, mixing thoroughly. Pour the mixture into an ovenproof dish and sprinkle the remaining cheese over the top.

6. Bake for 15 minutes. Remove from the oven and serve.

7. Fine to freeze. Defrost naturally and reheat in a 200°C (180°C fan) oven for 15 minutes.

Dinners

cheesy veg patties

Makes
5

Egg-free and containing four of your five fruit and veg a day, this quick and delicious meal needs to be tried to be believed!

1 handful of grated carrot

1 handful of grated courgette

1 handful of grated cheese (any type)

1 avocado, peeled and de-stoned

1 cup (125g) plain flour

For cooking
sunflower oil

1. Mix all the ingredients, except the oil, in a bowl until well combined, then divide and roll into 5 patties.

2. Heat a good glug of oil in a frying pan over a medium heat. When hot, add the patties and fry for 5 minutes on each side.

3. Pat with kitchen paper to remove any excess oil, then serve.

4. Fine to freeze. Defrost naturally and reheat in the microwave for 30 seconds, or eat cold.

florentine pizza

There was a time when Harry wouldn't eat spinach. Then, I tried chucking it on a tortilla bread with some cheese and an egg and I called it pizza. I'm sure you can guess what happened next or you wouldn't be reading about it now! I make this for myself and/or Tom for lunch when Harry is at school, because we all love it and this is one that Harry actually requests now. Spinach has well and truly been welcomed back into his realm it seems!

1 tbsp cream cheese

1 tortilla wrap

2 handfuls of spinach

1 handful of grated cheese (any type)

1 egg

1. Preheat the oven to 200°C (180°C fan). Line a baking tray with baking paper.

2. Spread the cream cheese over the tortilla wrap, then sprinkle the spinach in a ring around the outside. Sprinkle the cheese over the whole thing, then crack the egg into the middle.

3. Place the pizza on the prepared tray and bake for 10 minutes.

4. Remove from the oven and leave to cool for a few minutes before serving.

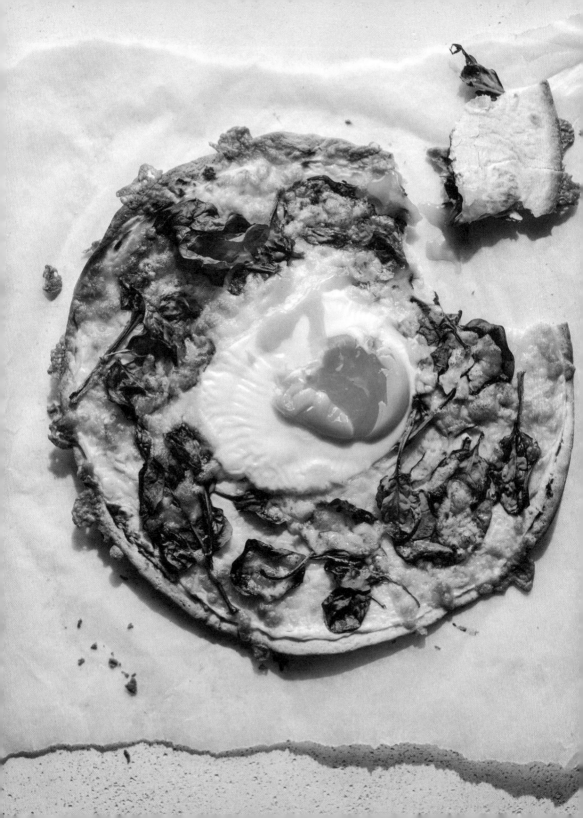

spring risotto

Serves 1

A fresh, vibrant bowl of comforting risotto with lots of green goodness in it. This is a one-pan wonder, so there's minimal washing up and leftovers can be turned into arancini balls (see Tip).

2 spring onions, chopped

½ cup (95g) arborio or other risotto rice

285ml low-salt vegetable stock

½ courgette, grated

1 handful of peas (fresh or frozen)

For cooking

1 tsp butter or olive oil

1. Heat the butter or oil in a saucepan over a low heat, then add the spring onions and cook until softened.

2. Add the rice and toast it gently. Once you can hear it pop slightly and you can smell toasted rice, add the veggie stock. Cook for 10 minutes, stirring the rice every couple of minutes to stop it from sticking. If it starts to catch on the bottom or dry out, add a little splash of water.

3. Add the grated courgette and cook for a further 10 minutes. Add the peas for the final minute to heat through.

4. Serve immediately.

To make into arancini balls, let the risotto cool. Rub olive oil into your hands and roll the mixture into balls about the same size as golf balls. Take 3 bowls, crack an egg into one and beat it, add a few tbsp of plain flour to another, and sprinkle a good handful of breadcrumbs into the third bowl. Take a ball and drop it into the flour, then into the egg mixture and then the breadcrumbs. Repeat this process until all are coated. Shallow-fry them in a little oil over a medium heat until golden and crispy. Pop them on a plate lined with kitchen paper to absorb any excess oil and that's it.

Dinners

Six

Desserts

Desserts

Most evenings, Harry has some fruit or a yoghurt for pudding, but occasionally I will make him something a bit more substantial – usually at the weekend or if I have time. I don't have much of a sweet tooth, but this is not something my son and I share! All of these dishes are fruit-based and certainly aren't packed with sugar. If Harry had his own way, he would choose chocolate ice cream for breakfast, lunch and dinner, but I haven't given into his astonishingly frequent requests for it yet! Never say never.

cereal ice cream

I can just imagine your puzzled expression, as it does sound strange, but this recipe was a bit of a breakthrough for me. As I may have mentioned before, Harry is borderline obsessed with ice cream, and this healthy version has hit the spot on countless occasions. I usually top it with fresh fruit, arm him with a spoon and wait patiently for the inevitable, 'Mummy, can I have some more please?'

3 ripe bananas

2 wheat biscuits (such as Weetabix)

1 cup (250ml) milk

1. Peel the bananas and add them to a blender along with the wheat biscuits and milk. Blitz until smooth, then pour into a freezerproof container.

2. Freeze for at least 8 hours.

Desserts

cherry and coconut pancakes

Makes
8–10

These decadent pancakes make a great fruity dessert. Not only do they look beautiful but the coconut makes them seem almost exotic! I plonk a few mashed cherries and a drizzle of syrup on top, or perhaps a little blob of cherry jam with some extra coconut, and they go down a treat.

1 cup (130g) self-raising flour

1 cup (250ml) milk (any type)

1 egg

1 handful of chopped cherries

2 tbsp desiccated coconut

For cooking
drizzle of sunflower oil

1. Combine all the ingredients, except the oil, in a bowl and mix thoroughly.

2. Heat a drizzle of oil in a frying pan over a medium heat. Ladle in small amounts of the mixture and fry each pancake for a few minutes on each side until golden.

3. Fine to freeze. Defrost naturally and reheat on a plate in the microwave for 20 seconds.

Desserts

berry jellies

If you are having a little party or perhaps just fancy making something a bit healthier than plain jelly to go with ice cream, then try this recipe. It's also a great way to preserve some fresh berries for a few days longer.

1 packet of jelly
(flavour and type of
your choice)

1 handful of fresh berries
(raspberries work best)

1. Mix up the jelly mixture according to the packet instructions.

2. Pop a berry into each individual section of an ice-cube tray. Pour over the warm jelly mixture and pop the ice-cube tray into the fridge for a minimum of 8 hours to set.

3. That's it!

4. Fine to freeze. Make sure you defrost fully before serving (they are impossible to bite into frozen – I nearly lost a tooth trying, because the outside turns to jelly but the fruit inside stays frozen!).

Desserts

plum crumble

Serves
2

Harry and I found a wild plum tree when out walking a couple of years ago. We picked so many plums I didn't know what to do with them. Harry loves plums so that wasn't the problem, but they don't last long and I didn't want to waste any of them. I made a huge plum crumble, which we had after our Sunday lunch and it was so delicious that the following week Harry and I had to go back and pick more.

1 handful of porridge oats

pinch of ground cinnamon

1 handful of finely chopped plums

2 tbsp apple sauce

1 tbsp raisins

pinch of brown sugar (optional)

1. Preheat the oven to 200°C (180°C fan). Line a baking tray with baking paper.

2. Sprinkle the oats onto the baking tray and sprinkle the cinnamon over the top. Bake for 10 minutes.

3. Meanwhile, spoon the chopped plums, apple sauce and raisins into a small ovenproof dish.

4. Remove the toasted oats from the oven and sprinkle them over the plum mixture. If you want some additional sweetness, you can sprinkle a pinch of brown sugar on top of the oats at this point.

5. Bake for 20 minutes and serve warm.

6. Fine to freeze. Ideally, freeze before baking. Bake from frozen in a 200°C (180°C fan) oven for 25 minutes. Of course, it can be frozen after it has been cooked but it will need to cool completely before freezing, then defrost naturally and reheat in the oven for just 10 minutes.

grape granita

Grapes are naturally very sweet and delicious, but they are just about the most well-known choking hazard there is. However, I didn't want Harry to miss out on them so I used to freeze them and whizz them up. You'd think this was absolutely packed with sugar, but as you can see from the ingredients – it's literally JUST grapes. A great way to give little ones a taste!

1 bunch of seedless grapes

2 tbsp water

1. Pluck all the grapes off the stalks and pop them into a sandwich bag. Freeze overnight or for at least 8 hours.

2. The next day, add them to a blender with the water and blitz to combine.

3. Serve immediately.

banana biscuit pudding

Serves
1

'Can I have pudding?'
'Yes, you can have a banana.'
'I don't want a banana, I want a PROPER pudding.'
And this was how banana biscuit pudding was born!

1 wheat biscuit
(such as Weetabix)

1 tbsp apple sauce

2 ripe bananas, plus
extra to serve (optional)

2 tbsp natural yoghurt

1. Crumble the wheat biscuit into a bowl, then mix in the apple sauce. Pack the mixture into the bottom of a cup using the back of a spoon.

2. Mash the bananas in another bowl, then mix in the yoghurt. Spoon this mixture over the top of the biscuit base.

3. Refrigerate for up to 1 hour, then serve, topped with extra banana slices, if you like.

Desserts

tropical vegan ice-cream

Serves

12

This is perhaps more a sorbet than an ice cream, but it's absolutely delicious and perfect on a hot summer's day to cool down any little paddling-pool enthusiasts!

½ x 400g tin of full-fat coconut milk

2 good handfuls of frozen mango chunks

1. Add both ingredients to a blender and blitz until smooth.

2. That really is it! Serve immediately.

3. Freezes for up to 6 months. Will need to soften for 20 minutes at room temperature before serving.

Tip

You can swap the mango for frozen pineapple, melon, banana or berries.

Desserts

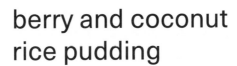

berry and coconut rice pudding

Serves 1

I must admit, I'm not a big fan of rice pudding. It always seems a little... bland, for my liking. It's creamy and sweet though, so most children enjoy it. By adding some berries and some coconut it turns into the most amazingly vibrant and vitamin-rich little dessert that adults and children can both enjoy.

3 tbsp arborio or pudding rice

180ml full-fat coconut milk

1 handful of blueberries

1 tsp jam (flavour of your choice)

1. Preheat the oven to 200°C (180°C fan).

2. Combine all the ingredients in a small ovenproof dish or ramekin. Cover with foil or add the lid if the dish has one.

3. Bake for 30 minutes.

4. Remove from the oven, remove the lid or foil, and leave to stand for 10 minutes for it to thicken and cool down.

5. Serve!

banana hearts

Serves
4

Three ingredients, pretty as a picture, sticky and naturally sweet – what's not to enjoy?!

3 very ripe bananas

1 glug of milk (any type), plus extra for brushing

1 sheet of ready-made puff pastry

1. Preheat the oven to 200°C (180°C fan). Line a baking tray with baking paper.

2. Mash the bananas in a bowl, adding a small glug of milk to loosen the mixture until it is a spreadable texture.

3. Unroll the sheet of puff pastry, pour the banana mixture onto it and use a palette or butter knife to spread the mixture over the whole sheet. Roll the two long sides of the pastry sheet in towards each other. Slice the roll into 3cm-thick slices and place each one flat on the baking tray (leaving a little space between them). Brush each one with a little milk.

4. Bake for 30 minutes.

5. Remove from the oven and leave to cool before serving.

6. If freezing, freeze the slices before cooking in between sheets of greaseproof paper. Cook from frozen as above, adding an extra 10 minutes to the cooking time.

raspberry and chocolate mousse

Serves 1

Chocolate mousse is probably on most children's pudding wish list, and frankly I don't blame them! However, this version is much healthier and miles easier to make at home. The pectin in the raspberries helps these to set and a few chocolate shavings across the top mean that, if you're anything like me, you'll probably need to photograph this little masterpiece once you've made it, because it looks almost as good as it tastes!

1 handful of raspberries

1 tsp cocoa powder

5 pitted Medjool dates

1 banana

a little splash of milk (any type)

To decorate *(optional)*
chocolate shavings

more raspberries

1. Combine all the ingredients in a blender or food processor and blitz until smooth.

2. Pour the mixture into a small cup or jar and refrigerate for at least 1 hour before serving.

3. Add some chocolate shavings and a raspberry or two to the top to decorate, if you like.

sweet potato chocolate brownies

Makes
12

The texture of these is similar to that of the most butter-filled sumptuous brownie you could buy from a farm shop or deli. But that's nothing to do with complicated process or pounds of unsalted butter – it's the work of that well-known orange superfood, the sweet potato! These are also very nice if you pop them in the freezer and eat them like ice cream!

2 sweet potatoes

2 tbsp coconut oil, softened

1 cup (130g) self-raising flour

3 tbsp cocoa powder

3 eggs

To decorate *(optional)*
melted chocolate

1. Preheat the oven to 200°C (180°C fan). Line a 25 x 16.5 x 3.5cm baking tin with baking paper.

2. Bake the sweet potatoes in the oven for 40 minutes, or until soft.

3. Remove the sweet potatoes from the oven and scoop the flesh out into a bowl. Mash it, then leave it to cool.

4. When cool, add the sweet potato mash to a blender or food processor along with the other ingredients and blitz to combine.

5. Pour the mixture into the prepared tin and bake for 30 minutes.

6. Remove from the oven and leave to cool for 20 minutes before slicing into squares.

7. If you'd like to make these extra sweet, you can drizzle the brownies with melted chocolate when cool.

Desserts

blueberry and peanut butter cups

These sticky little desserts would make a perfect breakfast, snack or special treat because the rich peanut butter, toasted oats and earthy blueberries make it taste like it's a 'proper pudding', to quote my son, when in fact these are basically the makings of a bowl of healthy porridge!

1 cup (100g) porridge oats

3 tbsp (50ml) milk (any type)

1 banana

1 handful of blueberries

1 tbsp peanut butter (any type)

For greasing
butter

1. Preheat the oven to 200°C (180°C fan). Grease a 6-hole muffin tin with a little butter.

2. Combine all the ingredients in a bowl and mix until well combined.

3. Spoon the mixture into the holes of the muffin tin and squash down with the back of a spoon.

4. Bake for 30 minutes.

5. Remove from the oven and leave to cool before popping them out to serve.

6. Fine to freeze. Defrost naturally before serving.

fruit lollies

Serves

4

These aren't sugar-free, of course, but make a lovely refreshing snack. They look just like chocolate lollies, but include a lot more goodness. Watermelon is probably up there as a favourite fruit for lots of people, but they are absolutely enormous and impossible to store if you buy them whole, or gone in seconds if you buy the snack pots or packets. This way, you can eke out those precious slices for a little longer or preserve the leftovers if you've invested in a whole one, and pack your freezer with healthy lollies for many desserts to come! I use pre-sliced watermelon fingers for this. You can buy them in most supermarkets and they are deseeded, which makes things much easier.

100g white or milk chocolate, as you like

1 tbsp coconut oil

lollipop sticks

watermelon fingers (bought ready-sliced or make your own cut into 10 x 2 x 2cm sticks)

1. Place the chocolate and coconut oil in a microwaveable bowl. Melt in the microwave on high power for 1 minute, pausing every 20 seconds to stir it.

2. Insert a lollipop stick into one end of each watermelon finger.

3. Once the chocolate is melted, dip each watermelon finger in the chocolate and turn until coated.

4. Pop each lolly on a plate covered in clingfilm and freeze for a minimum of 8 hours.

Tip

I also love to make mango lollies in exactly the same way. So pretty!

226

Desserts

bramble cheesecake bars

Picking blackberries or brambles is a classic way to kill a few hours on a warm late summer's afternoon, but then what do you do with them? This a great way to use up your surplus and get the little ones involved with mashing (they love mashing things, don't they?!) to produce a yummy, healthy pudding. If you want to freeze these, they are even less messy, and possibly even better, partially frozen/defrosted as a sort of iced cake bar.

6 tbsp unsalted butter

2 wheat biscuits
(such as Weetabix)

3 heaped tbsp cream cheese

2 handfuls of brambles
(blackberries, raspberries, dewberries)

1 tsp raspberry jam

1. Line a dish or tin (about 18 x 11.5 x 4cm) with baking paper.

2. Melt 3 tablespoons of the butter in a bowl (either in the microwave or in a pan, then pour into a bowl). Crumble the wheat biscuits into the bowl and mix thoroughly.

3. Pack the mixture into the bottom of the lined dish and use the back of a spoon to flatten it.

4. Pop the dish in the fridge for 10 minutes to set.

5. Meanwhile, combine the remaining 3 tablespoons of butter in a separate bowl with the cream cheese, brambles and jam until well combined.

6. Spoon the mixture on top of the wheat-biscuit base and smooth it out.

7. Freeze for at least 2 hours, then slice into squares to serve.

8. These will keep for up to 48 hours in the fridge in a sealed container, but they will be very soft. For a firmer bar, they are fine to freeze. Remove from the freezer a few minutes before you want to serve them – they are nice to eat while still partially frozen as a sort of ice-cream bar.

Desserts

fudgy banana and chocolate flapjacks

Makes

12

I don't know why, but ripe bananas cooked in this way have the taste and texture of fudge, which is definitely a bonus! These are nice hot or cold, they make a great dessert, snack or breakfast, and it saves you worrying about whether the kids will turn their nose up at a slightly brown, mushy banana, because the more ripe the banana, the sweeter the end result!

4 bananas, plus extra, sliced, to decorate (optional)

2 cups (200g) porridge oats

1 cup (250ml) milk (any type)

1 tbsp chocolate spread, plus extra to decorate

2 handfuls of chopped dates

1. Preheat the oven to 200°C (180°C fan). Line a 25 x 16.5 x 3.5cm baking tray with baking paper.

2. Mash the bananas in a bowl, then add the oats, milk, chocolate spread and chopped dates, and mix to combine.

3. Pour the mixture into the prepared tray.

4. Bake for 45 minutes.

5. Remove from the oven and leave to cool before slicing and serving.

6. Fine to freeze. Defrost naturally before serving.

 Add an extra splodge of chocolate spread to the top to decorate, for a naughty treat, or some fresh banana slices make for a healthier topping.

Desserts

Meal Planner Template

Here is a handy meal planner template. Ideal for planning out your own menus, once you've worked out what works for your own little one/s. Photocopy it and stick it to your fridge for easy reference.

	Breakfast	Savoury Sna
M		
T		
W		
Th		
F		
Sat		
Sun		

Lunch	Sweet Snack	Dinner	Dessert

Index

Acknowledgements

Thank you to my amazing family who have supported and encouraged me every step of the way. Special thanks to my mum for being my biggest advocate and loving cheerleader, and for being, without a doubt, more optimistic about all this at every stage than perhaps I was. To my dad, for always inspiring and continuing to inspire my passion for food from day dot! To my wonderful friends, and specifically Chloe, who actually pushed me to start an Instagram page in the first place.

Thank you to my amazing agent Juliet, who calmed my nerves and neuroses more often than she realised and who I am delighted to now call my friend. She saw exactly what I wanted, exactly as I saw it and kept me sane along the way. A huge thank you to HQ, specifically Kate Fox, Nira Begum and Louise McKeever, who have all been my editor at some point during this process, for taking my vision and turning it into this beautiful book. Special thanks to Emily Preece-Morrison for overseeing the entire editorial process and pulling everything together so expertly, and to Nikki Dupin for designing every single page!

To the wonderful team who directed, cooked, photographed and curated the beautiful images in these pages: Liz and Max Haarala-Hamilton, Aya Nishimura, Rosie Reynolds and Troy Willis.

Massive thanks to my amazing Instagram friends and followers (the Dorises!), without whom none of this would have happened. I might have given you some simple recipes to feed your little ones, but in return I have gained self-confidence, a dream, a career and a sense of belonging. Particular thanks to Mrs Hinch, who quite literally changed the direction of my life and in whose journal I wrote down my goal 'to publish a cookbook' long before I started my food page – and here we are!

Finally, and most importantly, thank you to Tom and Harry. When I asked Harry if I should go and be a teacher or do 'the cooking thing', he replied, 'the cooking one Mummy, because I really like your food and you can be at home with me.' He knew what was best for me when I wasn't sure myself. And to Tom, whose belief in me was fiercer than anyone's, especially my own, and who genuinely held the strings of our lives together single-handedly so that I could follow my passion. I'm truly and forever grateful.

HQ
An imprint of HarperCollinsPublishers Ltd
1 London Bridge Street
London SE1 9GF

www.harpercollins.co.uk

HarperCollinsPublishers
Macken House, 39/40 Mayor Street Upper,
Dublin 1, D01 C9W8, Ireland

10 9 8 7 6 5 4 3 2

First published in Great Britain by
HQ, an imprint of HarperCollinsPublishers Ltd 2022

ISBN: 978-0-00-850929-3

Printed and bound in Latvia by PNB

Photographer: Haarala Hamilton Photography
Art Direction and Design: Nic & Lou
Senior Editor: Nira Begum
Project Editor: Emily Preece-Morrison
Senior Production Controller: Halema Begum